COSMIC CUISINE

COSMIC CUISINE

The Astrological Cookbook

Tom Jaine

&

Nicholas Campion

WINDWARD

Published by Windward
an imprint owned by W H Smith Limited
Registered No. 237811, England
Trading as WHS Distributors
St John's House, East Street, Leicester, LE1 6NE

This book was created and produced by
Roxby General Books Limited
A division of Roxby Press Limited
126 Victoria Rise
London SW4 0NW
United Kingdom

Editor: Rachel Grenfell
Design: Eric Drewery & Adrian Singer
& Direct Input Ltd
Photography: Jhon Kevern
Home economist: Stella Joyce
Stylist: Valerie Kevern, Tables Laid
Typesetting: TND Serif Limited
Origination: HILO Offset Limited

ISBN 0-7112-0564-7

Printed and bound in Yugoslavia
by Mladinska knjiga, Ljubljana

CONTENTS

Introduction   6

Tables of Correspondences   9

SUN SIGNS

Aries   12
Aries — *Recipes*   14

Taurus   20
Taurus — *Recipes*   22

Gemini   28
Gemini — *Recipes*   30

Cancer   36
Cancer — *Recipes*   38

Leo   44
Leo — *Recipes*   46

Virgo   52
Virgo — *Recipes*   54

Libra   60
Libra — *Recipes*   62

Scorpio   68
Scorpio — *Recipes*   70

Sagittarius   76
Sagittarius — *Recipes*   78

Capricorn   84
Capricorn — *Recipes*   86

Aquarius   92
Aquarius — *Recipes*   94

Pisces   100
Pisces — *Recipes*   102

PLANETARY PALATES

Sun   108
Sun — *Recipes*   110

Moon   114
Moon — *Recipes*   116

Mercury   120
Mercury — *Recipes*   122

Venus   126
Venus — *Recipes*   128

Mars   132
Mars — *Recipes*   134

Jupiter   138
Jupiter — *Recipes*   140

Saturn   144
Saturn — *Recipes*   146

Food for Love   150

Food for Profit   154

Food Index   158

Index   159

INTRODUCTION

Each sign of the Zodiac and each of the seven traditional planets that rule them — Uranus, Neptune and Pluto have not been included — has been accorded its own chapter. In every instance, the types of food, the ingredients, the style of cooking, the ambience and circumstance of eating that are preferred by, or associated with, the signs and planets have been noted. Nicholas Campion has also written a general introduction to each sign sketching the gastronomical tendencies, fads, likes and dislikes of its subjects. Read this and be ready for your guests!

The associations between astrology and food are firmly rooted in the ancient doctrine of correspondences, according to which all things in the universe, human, animal, vegetable, mineral and cosmic, are united in a vast web of interdependent relationships. To our forebears it made no difference whether these connections were grounded on physical fact or whether their existence was purely symbolic. The importance was that these relationships could be used as models for living. To them it was self-evident that, just as the fortunes of human beings could be read in the stars, so also could the patterns of nature. It was vital to take this simple truth into account and to live in harmony with nature and the cosmos.

Renaissance astrologers had an eye for detail that enabled them to move from grand philosophical speculations at one moment to formulating rules to determine the correct times to cut hair or toenails at the next. It was appropriate, therefore, to turn their attention to the natural world and assign a place to animals, fish, birds, plants, vegetables, herbs and fruit in the astrological scheme. Every identifiable item in nature was allotted a sign of the Zodiac or a planet, sometimes both, as its 'ruler', thereby relating various foods to specific seasons and time of day.

Human beings were given their rulerships, too. For anyone even remotely familiar with astrology it was possible to relate food to people by using the lists of correspondences. The modern aphorism 'you are what you eat' would have made perfect sense to people who grew up in a world where human beings saw themselves as part of the natural order.

If there is a general rule in Cosmic Cuisine it is that a sign of the Zodiac has influence over style, location, characteristics and even the geography of cookery and eating. The planets, however, are more specifically associated with the ingredients themselves. For example, a Libran meal may be characterized by harmony and amity, in a setting designed to induce mellowness. It could also draw on Chinese or other oriental inspiration to determine the shape and structure of the menu; but for guidance over which foods to serve, you should turn to the chapter relating to Libra's ruler, the planet Venus. There you will find suggestions on style and ambience, as also lists of meats, vegetables, fruit and herbs that are especially Venusian.

It is fortunate there is a degree of internal logic to the lists and pronouncements of early astrologers. The relationships of star signs to their planets make culinary sense, for the most part, even if the connections become quite complex when you try to sort out the shades of dryness or moisture associated with two signs under one planet.

The understanding that diet is of critical importance to our wellbeing, and that people have varying food requirements, has been claimed by the whole-food industry as its own. Yet the motivations of health food specialists are often deeply bound up with self-denial, and the belief that food is only pleasurable when it is healthy and only healthy when it is bland and plain. With one or two exceptions the gourmet and the gourmand are excluded from the world of contemporary holistic cuisine. The astrologer recognizes that such an unbalanced situation is symbolized by Saturn, ruler of hardship and discipline, and that in real life this planet should always be balanced by Jupiter, the ruler of freedom, which includes the freedom to enjoy our food.

Food can be a great healer, and there is little that has more power to boost flagging morale than a good, rich, tasty meal. The fifteenth century Florentine Renaissance philosopher, Marsillio Ficino, argued that the best cure for ailments induced by Saturn, such as depression, was a strong dose of the planet Venus, best achieved by eating and drinking to your heart's content, followed by a bout of dalliance with the opposite sex. Such behaviour, he mused, would cheer up all but those suffering from the most miserable complaints.

Each chapter contains a series of recipes which illustrate the principles described for a sign or planet. We have grouped these so that there are first courses, main courses, vegetables or vegetarian dishes and desserts in every chapter. There are also occasional extras — pickle recipes for the Moon, for instance.

It is rare for any recipe to consist solely of material, methods and style associated with a single sign or planet. Usually recipes are an astrological amalgam. Nonetheless, the choice of recipes has point and the specific reasons for putting them under a particular sign are touched on in the individual head-notes.

Nothing in the real world is ever simple for long, and in many cases the association between plant and sign, or plant and planet, is ambiguous. For example, Venus, it might be thought, is the natural ruler of the sweet and fleshy pineapple, yet this fruit is often placed under Mars, the ruler of spiky skins. The banana, another soft, fleshy and sweet candidate for Venus, may be placed under Mars, the planet of male sexuality, on account of its phallic shape, or the Sun because of its golden colour. Similarly, the Venusian orange is more often assigned to the Sun by virtue of its solar colour and shape.

The astrological cook is, therefore, accorded a convenient degree of latitude when it comes to selecting ingredients, and this creative flexibility is enhanced when the signs of the Zodiac are added to the scheme. Each sign has a special connection with, or is 'ruled' by, one of the planets. For example, Aries is ruled by Mars, so Mars' foods have a special place in the Arien repertoire and vice versa.

In large part, though not exclusively, astrology governs cooking by means of general principle rather than detailed recommendation. Once these principles have been grasped, it is not an impossibility to extend them to the construction of your own Cosmic Cuisine, rather than any slavish following of recipes and lists. For one, it would require a concordance of a thousand pages to locate every foodstuff known to man in its astrological context. When, therefore, you have an ingredient not mentioned in the lists below, you resort to principles for its placement: Mars rules all hot spices; Venus governs succulent fruit; Pisces is self-evidently in favour of fish; and so on (see Tables of Correspondences).

Using the stars as guide to your hours at the stove may take many forms. You may have Geminean guests: turn to Gemini and Mercury for ideas about setting and menu. You may have several guests, all of different star signs: compose a meal reflecting their individual characteristics. You are giving a meal with a particular end in view — a delicate negotiation, a reconciliation, a pursuit of love — consider then the signs and planets that influence these things: a warrior's Martian feast of chillis, pepper and fiery reds, will not induce that calm sense of well-being you may desire as you entertain some new object of your affections — turn to Libra, quickly. Some suggestions on planning a meal with a special purpose are indicated in the chapters on a lovers' feast and a business lunch. It is plain from these that ideas can be drawn from several signs and planets at once, that variety, here as everywhere, is the spice of life.

The recipes are collected from many sources, with a view to their astrological suitability: their relation to place, mood, or ingredient. Some are original (as far as is any recipe) others rely on literature and earlier cookery books.

TABLE OF CORRESPONDENCES FOR THE SIGNS

Sign	Ruling Planet	Element	Polarity	Quality	Part of Body	Colour	Food
ARIES	Mars	Fire	Positive	Cardinal, Hot, Dry	Head	Red	Fast Food
TAURUS	Venus	Earth	Negative	Fixed, Cold, Dry	Throat	Blues, Pinks, Greens	Dairy Products
GEMINI	Mercury	Air	Positive	Mutable, Hot, Wet	Hands, Arms, Lungs	Various	Fast Food
CANCER	Moon	Water	Negative	Cardinal, Cold, Wet	Breasts, Stomach	Silver, soft shades	Shellfish
LEO	Sun	Fire	Positive	Fixed, Hot, Dry	Heart, Spine	Gold, Scarlet	Rich Food
VIRGO	Mercury	Earth	Negative	Mutable, Cold, Dry	Intestines	Grey, Navy	Wholefood, Grains, Refined Food
LIBRA	Venus	Air	Positive	Cardinal, Hot, Wet	Kidneys	Blues, Pinks, Delicate Shades	Sweet, Delicate Food
SCORPIO	Mars	Water	Negative	Fixed, Cold, Wet	Reproductive Organs	Deep Red, Blue, Black	Mouldy or curdled Food (eg Blue cheese, Yoghurt)
SAGITTARIUS	Jupiter	Fire	Positive	Mutable, Hot	Thighs	Purple, Deep Blue	Fast Food
CAPRICORN	Saturn	Earth	Negative	Cardinal, Cold, Dry	Knees	Sober, Dark Colour	Traditional Dishes
AQUARIUS	Saturn	Air	Positive	Fixed, Hot, Wet	Ankles	Electric Blue	Unusual Food
PISCES	Jupiter	Water	Negative	Mutable, Cold, Wet	Feet	Turquoise, Sea-Green	Sea Food

TABLE OF CORRESPONDENCES FOR THE PLANETS

Planet	Corres-ponding Sign	Quality	Taste	Part of Body	Flowers	Trees	Colour	Metal	Precious Stone	Day of Week
SUN	Leo	hot and dry	aromatic, sweet and sour	heart and circulatory system	marigold, peony	walnut cedar, laurel cedar, orange, lemon	yellow, scarlet	gold	carbuncle, hyacinth	sunday
MOON	Cancer	cold and moist	juicy, slightly sweet	lymphatic and digestive system	wallflower, water lily, poppy, white rose	willow, linden	white pale yellow or green	silver	crystal	monday
MERCURY	Gemini and Virgo	cool and dry	varied, changeable	respiratory system	lavender, lily of the valley	mulberry, elder, walnut	dove-grey	mercury	topaz	wednesday
VENUS	Taurus and Libra	cool and moist	perfumed, sweet smelling	reproductive system	damask rose, cowslip, daisy, foxglove, violet	cherry, pear, apple	white, pale blue or green	copper	jade, emerald	friday
MARS		Aries and Scorpio	hot and dry	hot, dry	muscular system	anemone	chestnut	red	iron	diamond jasper	tuesday
JUPITER	Sagittarius and Pisces	warm and moist	sweet, scented fragant	liver	dandelion, red rose	cherry, chestnut, fig, maple, oak almond, pear	purple, sea-green azure	tin	amethyst emerald,	thursday
SATURN	Capricorn and Aquarius	cold and dry	sour, bitter, sharp	skin, bone structure	wild campion	pine, beech holly, poplar, quince cypress, yew	dull, dark and sober, grey, brown	lead	sapphire, lapis lazuli	saturday

nimals	Birds	Fish	Fruit & Nuts	Vegetables, grains etc.	Herbs, Spices and Flavourings etc.
orse, ram, ull, goat, mb, cks			orange, lemon, pomegranates, olives, all nuts	barley, rice, maize, sugar cane	camomile, saffron, turmeric, rosemary, cinnamon, mustard, sage, ginger, lovage, mace, nutmeg, peppermint, vervain, sunflower seeds
og, snail, icken, bbit, ttle, g (ham)	geese, duck	all shellfish and fish	melons	cabbage family, marrow family, chicory, endive, mushrooms, potato, tomato, watercress, cucumber, seaweed, lettuce, barley	rosemary, hyssop, poppy seeds
are nison		mullet	mulberry, hazelnut, walnut	carrot, celery, fennel, beans, oats	savory, fennel seed, caraway, dill, parsley, vervain, fenugreek, liquorice, marjoram, treacle
er, young ttle, at, bbit	chicken, partridge, dove		all soft fruit including currants and berries, apples, pears, oranges, dates, grapes, mangoes, olives, raisins, almonds	artichokes, asparagus, beans, parsnip, sorrel, dandelion, buckwheat, millet, rye, wheat	dandelion, fenugreek, thyme, coriander, cloves, parsley, yarrow, linden flower, oregano, peppermint, savory, vervain
at		shark, pike	barberry, pineapple, rhubarb	capsicum, onion, leek, aubergine, nettles, radish	capers, chives, rue, chilli, pepper, tamarind, basil, cayenne, horseradish, garlic, ginger, mustard, coffee, tea, hops
eep, deer	partridge, pheasant chicken dove	shark, tuna	almond, apple, apricot, bilberry, currants, raisins, strawberry, orange, rhubarb	asparagus, chicory, endive, leek, tomato, turnip, parsnip, chickpeas, rice, barley, wheat, sugar cane	aniseed, borage, chervil, cinnamon, cloves, hyssop, nutmeg, mint, peppermint, spearmint, jasmine, thyme, sage, sesame, maple syrup, sugar, ginseng
g		shellfish	quince, olive, sloe	parsnip, spinach, onion, beetroot, potato, lentils, barley	capers, comfrey, sage, cumin, coriander, vervain, carob, coffee, gelatine

ARIES

SUN IN ARIES 21 MARCH - 19 APRIL
RULED BY MARS

ARIES is the first sign of the Zodiac and Ariens have a reputation as innovators and leaders in their chosen field. Ruled by Mars, the classical god of war, this is the most direct and energetic of all the signs. It is fiery, hot, dry and masculine.

ARIES ENVIRONMENTS
Traditionally Ariens love bright, noisy places and all the bustle of a crowded restaurant. Yet the fact that they are often worn out from overwork means that Ariens frequently prefer a quiet place in which they can relax and recharge their batteries. They have a high metabolic rate and tend to eat their food too quickly, ignoring the subtleties of taste. For them an open fire provides the perfect atmosphere for an intimate meal.

ARIES FOODS
Food prepared quickly or cooked at the table suits the Arien love of speed, and as a hot-dry sign baked or barbecued food is appropriate. Lamb, venison and goat are all ruled by this sign. Aries itself does not rule any fruit or vegetables, although those ruled by Mars are associated with it.

SWEDISH SALT HERRING GRATIN
Serves Four

This dish is often part of a Swedish *smörgåsbord*, that grand array of hot and cold food laid out for special occasions. It can also be served as a first course to a dinner or as a light lunch dish. Serve a bowl of sour cream flavoured with dill as an accompaniment.

4 fillets salt herring
4 medium potatoes
2 large onions
4 oz/125g butter
black pepper
2 oz/50g soft breadcrumbs

Soak the fillets for 12 hours in 2 or 3 changes of cold water. Lift out, pat dry and remove skins. Peel and slice the potatoes and onions thinly. Butter an oval or oblong baking dish and arrange crosswise rows of potatoes, herring and onions. Season with freshly ground black pepper. Cover with breadcrumbs and dot with butter. Cook at the top of a preheated oven at 400°F/200°C/ Gas Mark 6 for 30 minutes. Reduce to 325°F/ 160°C/Gas Mark 3 for another 20 minutes.

TOMATOES STUFFED WITH CREAM CHEESE AND BASIL
Serves Four

Mars has rule over basil, the king of herbs, as well as over tomatoes, basil's natural partner.

4 large beefsteak or Marmande tomatoes
salt
8 oz/225g cottage cheese
2 teaspoons grated Parmesan cheese
3 tablespoons soft breadcrumbs
1 tablespoon chopped basil
2 egg yolks
black pepper
butter

Cut the tops off the tomatoes and hollow out the insides. Dry the shells by sprinkling with salt and leaving upside down on the draining board for 10 minutes.

Sieve the cottage cheese and mix with the Parmesan, 2 tablespoons breadcrumbs, basil and egg yolks. Season with pepper. Fill the tomatoes with the mixture and place on a greased oven dish. Sprinkle the rest of the breadcrumbs on top and dot with butter. Bake in a preheated oven at 350°F/180°C/Gas Mark 4 for 15 to 20 minutes until cooked. Serve hot, warm or cool.

FALAFEL FROM ISRAEL
Serves Four to Eight

Israeli falafel are made with chick peas rather than dried broad beans as in Egypt. Here is truly Arien food. Serve them with a tomato salad dressed with parsley and chopped black olives.

6 oz/175g chick peas
1 small red onion
1 small clove garlic
1 oz/25g soft breadcrumbs
½ teaspoon ground coriander
good pinch baking powder
salt and black pepper
1 teaspoon ground cumin
oil for deep frying

Soak the chick peas in cold water for 24 to 36 hours. Rinse, drain and blend to a fine purée in a food processor.

Peel and cut up the onion and garlic. Add them to the purée and process again. Add the breadcrumbs, coriander, baking powder, salt and pepper and process a third time. Leave in a covered bowl for 30 to 60 minutes.

Shape the mixture into small balls 1 inch/2.5cm across and roll them in the ground cumin. Fry a few at a time in a deep fryer set at 375°F/190°C for 3 to 4 minutes, until golden. Serve immediately.

ANCHOIADE — ANCHOVY TOAST
Serves Four

This salty appetizer from Provence is good with drinks before a meal or served as a first course with some sticks of raw celery.

20 anchovy fillets
2 cloves garlic
black pepper

3 tablespoons good olive oil
1 teaspoon white wine vinegar
thinly sliced bread for toasting

Soak the anchovies for 5 minutes in cold water. Drain and pat dry. Pound with the garlic and black pepper in a mortar until a thick paste. Gradually add the oil, then the vinegar, pounding all the while.

Toast the bread on one side, spread with the paste on the other and grill until browned.

LAMBS' KIDNEYS IN BAKED POTATO JACKETS
Serves Four

Eat this dish on its own, but follow it up with mixed vegetables left to cool then dressed with oil and lemon.
4 large potatoes
4 oz/125g shallots
2 oz/50g butter
4 fl oz/120ml red wine
4 lambs' kidneys
4 oz/125g mushrooms
salt and black pepper
1 juniper berry, crushed
4 tablespoons double cream

Bake the potatoes in a preheated oven at 400°F/200°C/Gas Mark 6 for 1 hour. Cut their tops off. Hollow out the skins and mash the flesh. Reserve everything while cooking the kidneys.

Peel and chop the shallots and fry in half the butter. When cooked, add the red wine and reduce fiercely to a syrupy glaze.

Skin, core and slice the kidneys; wipe and slice the mushrooms. In another pan, fry the kidneys lightly in the rest of the butter. Add the mushrooms. When lightly cooked, season with salt and pepper and the crushed juniper berry. Add the shallots.

Half fill the potato skins with the mashed potato and spoon the kidneys on top. Put a spoonful of cream on each potato and replace their 'hats'. Bake in a preheated oven at 350°F/180°C/Gas Mark 4 until thoroughly hot.

ROAST LEG OF KID, TUSCAN STYLE
Serves Four

You can use small lamb instead of kid if that is unobtainable, but kid — infant of the sign itself — is most apt. Serve with roast potatoes and a purée of peas or, if you are feeling hungry, the Tuscan Fried Artichokes, on page 25.
1 leg of kid, about 3-4 lbs/1.4-1.8kg
2 cloves garlic
2 sprigs rosemary
salt and pepper
olive oil
8 fl oz/250ml dry white wine
3 oz/75g butter
lemon juice

Have the butcher bone the leg of kid. Peel and crush the garlic; strip the rosemary from its stalks. Spread the inside of the leg with the garlic and rosemary. Season with salt and pepper. Tie the leg up and rub it with oil. Put on a rack in an oven pan. Roast in a preheated oven at 425°F/220°C/ Gas Mark 7 for 15 minutes per pound, basting regularly with its juices.

When it is cooked, leave it to rest in a warm place on a serving dish for at least 15 minutes.

Drain off the fat from the roasting pan. Put the pan over heat. Add the white wine and bring to the boil stirring and scraping. Boil to reduce then whisk in the butter a little at a time. Check for seasoning, adding lemon juice if need be. Strain into a sauceboat and serve the sauce separately.

SHELLFISH PILAFF AS IN MARSEILLE
Serves Four

Offer the pilaff with a green salad with a chive dressing.
36 mussels
12 clams
1 onion
1 leek
1 tomato
4 tablespoons olive oil
6 large prawns or frozen *crevettes roses*
8 oz/225g risotto rice

2 cloves garlic, chopped
pinch saffron
bouquet garni
½ pint/300ml boiling water
1 bunch chives, chopped
black pepper

Wash and clean the mussels and clams. Cook them with 2 tablespoons of water in a large covered pan over high heat (you may have to do them in batches). Cook them for 5 to 8 minutes or until they open. Strain the cooking liquor through a fine sieve and reserve. Remove the mussels and clams from their shells and reserve.

Peel and chop the onion; wash, trim and slice the leek finely; skin, seed and chop the tomato. Heat the olive oil in a wide pan and cook the onion and leek without colouring. Add the tomato to the pan along with the prawns, rice, garlic and saffron. Fry some more, until the rice takes on a translucent look. Add the bouquet of herbs. Pour the boiling water into the pan. Simmer, uncovered, over low heat. Take care it does not stick.

When the water has been absorbed, add a cupful of the mussel liquor. Allow that to be absorbed then add some more and so on until the rice is cooked in about 20 to 30 minutes. Add the reserved mussels and clams, sprinkle with the chopped chives and some black pepper. Serve immediately.

LAMB KORMA WITH SPINACH
Serves Four to Six
Afghan cooking borrows from the Persian and the Indian tradition, though the spicing tends to be simpler than on the subcontinent. Serve this dish with some rice and a bowl of yoghurt seasoned with dried mint and salt and pepper. A sweet chutney would also be good.
1 tablespoon whole cumin seed
1 onion
2 cloves garlic
1 fresh chilli
1½ lb/700g boned trimmed lamb, cut in
    ¾ inch/2cm cubes

3 fl oz/85ml oil
salt and black pepper
1 tablespoon ground coriander
2 lb/900g spinach
3 tablespoons chopped fresh coriander
5 fl oz/150ml double cream

Put a heavy casserole on medium heat and put in the cumin. Roast, stirring, for about 2 minutes, until it begins to brown.

Peel and chop the onion and garlic; seed and chop the chilli. Put the oil in the casserole with the cumin and add the onion. Fry until brown. Season the lamb. Put the garlic, chilli, meat and ground coriander in the casserole and fry to brown all over. Add water to cover and bring to the boil. Cover the casserole and simmer over very low heat for about 45 minutes or until the meat is tender.

Wash and strip the spinach, draining well. Add to the casserole, with the chopped fresh coriander. Cook for 10 minutes, uncovered, over high heat, evaporating much of the liquid. Taste for seasoning.

Stir in the double cream and bubble up before serving.

NORTH AFRICAN SALAD
Serves Four
2 green peppers
2 cooking tomatoes
1 sweet onion
1 clove garlic
juice of ½ lemon
5 tablespoons olive oil
salt and black pepper
¼ teaspoon ground caraway seed
¼ teaspoon ground coriander
pinch chilli powder
1 tablespoon capers
12 black olives
1 tablespoon chopped parsley
1 small tin tuna
2 hard-boiled eggs, quartered

Grill the peppers, tomatoes, onion and garlic until the skins are well browned and blistered.

Remove their skins while they are still hot. Seed the peppers and tomatoes. Chop all together very finely.

Make a dressing of the lemon juice, oil, salt and spices.

Chop the capers and stone the olives. Mix everything together except the tuna and the eggs. Put the tuna in the centre of a dish. Arrange the dressed chopped vegetables around the tuna with the quartered eggs on the outside.

Lamb Korma with Spinach

POTATO GRIDDLE CAKES
Serves Four

These are eaten all over northern Europe and Scandinavia, often served with a fruit jelly or sauce: cold apple sauce, cranberries, or Swedish linganberries. They can be served as a course on their own, after a substantial soup, or as a vegetable with some light meat or egg dish.

2 lb/900g potatoes
2 eggs

salt and pepper

oil and lard or butter for shallow frying

Peel the potatoes. Set the largest one to cook in boiling salted water. When cooked, drain and mash. Grate the other potatoes on a coarse grater. Mix them with the eggs, mashed potato and seasoning.

Drop spoonfuls into a frying pan containing a mixture of hot oil and lard or oil and butter. Flatten them into cakes with the back of a spatula. Cook over a medium heat until golden brown. Turn, cook the other side.

LEEKS WITH LEMON AND SUGAR
Serves Four

This dish from Iran may be thought Venusian in its balance of the sugar with the tartness of the lemon. This can be eaten hot or cold.

8 leeks

1 clove garlic

1 tablespoon sugar

2 tablespoons oil

juice of 1 lemon

Wash the leeks well and dry. Cut them into broad slices. Crush the garlic with the flat of a knife. Cook the garlic with the sugar in the oil until the sugar lightly caramelizes. Add the leeks and the lemon juice. Cover the pan tightly and simmer until tender.

MAPLE GLAZED ONIONS
Serves Four

1 lb/450g pickling onions

salt

1 oz/25g butter

2 tablespoons good stock

2 tablespoons maple syrup

Peel the onions. Parboil them in salted water for about 10 minutes. Drain and turn them into a heavy pan with the butter, stock and maple syrup. Finish cooking over a medium heat, stirring to prevent sticking, for about 10 minutes until the glaze has been absorbed.

A SANDWICH SPREAD FROM EASTERN EUROPE
Serves Four

This can be spread on toast for a simple light meal or stuffed into wedges of green pimento. Plain radishes are a good accompaniment.

4 oz/125g cream or cottage cheese

2 oz/50g butter

1 tablespoon sour cream

1 teaspoon caraway seeds

2 spring onions, chopped

1 teaspoon ground paprika

salt

wheat or rye bread for toasting, or rye crackers

Cream the cheese with the butter and sour cream. Mix in the remaining ingredients and salt to taste.

PEARS WITH A GINGER SPONGE
Serves at least Four

Although not hot and dry, as should be most Arien foods, this delicious sponge uses ginger to give it some spice.

Serve with a lightly whipped cream, flavoured with lemon and sugar.

For the pears

2 oz/50g unsalted butter plus extra for the tin

3 large pears

3 oz/75g brown sugar

juice of 1 lemon

For the sponge

4 oz/125g unsalted butter

4 oz/125g caster sugar

2 eggs

6 oz/175g self-raising flour

1 teaspoon baking powder

½ teaspoon ground ginger

4 pieces crystallized or preserved ginger

up to 5 fl oz/150ml milk

Grease an 8 inch/20cm cake tin with butter. Use a tin with a fixed base.

Peel, quarter and core the pears. Slice them lengthwise. Put the brown sugar, butter and lemon juice in a small saucepan. Heat gently to dissolve then boil vigorously for about 5 minutes to make a good syrup. Tightly arrange the pears in concentric circles in the bottom of the cake tin. Pour the syrup over them.

Make the sponge by creaming the butter and sugar until light. Beat in the eggs gradually. Sift in the flour, baking powder and ground ginger. Chop the crystallized ginger and fold into the mixture. Add enough milk to make a dropping consistency. Pour over the pears and bake in a preheated oven at 375°F/190°C/Gas Mark 5 for about 60 minutes.

Test with a skewer. Run a knife round the sides, then turn out and serve while still warm.

POLISH SHORTBREAD WITH A RED FRUIT FILLING
Serves Four to Six
4 oz/125g softened butter, plus extra for the tin
6 oz/175g flour
½ teaspoon baking powder
pinch salt
2 oz/50g caster sugar
1 tablespoon redcurrant jelly
6 oz/175g mixed fresh red fruits — wild strawberries, raspberries, redcurrants, cherries
For the meringue
2 egg whites
2 oz/50g caster sugar

Grease a 7 inch/18cm sponge tin with a little butter.

Sift together the flour, baking powder and salt. Add the softened butter and caster sugar. Knead into a dough. Spread the dough into the sponge tin, pressing into all the corners. Smooth the top. Prick with a fork. Bake in a preheated oven at 325°F/160°C/Gas Mark 3 for 40 minutes until lightly browned. Remove from the oven.

Melt the redcurrant jelly in a pan and spread on the shortbread. Dot with the red fruits.

Beat the egg whites until stiff. Add the sugar. Beat again until it forms firm peaks. Spread the meringue over the fruit, return to the oven and brown for about 10 minutes. Serve cool.

CHOCOLATE STRAWBERRIES WITH CREAM AND PINEAPPLE
Serves Four
4 oz/125g bitter chocolate
3 teaspoons kirsch
16 large strawberries with stalks, cleaned
6 fl oz/175ml whipping cream
1 teaspoon icing sugar
1 teaspoon vanilla sugar
4 slices fresh ripe pineapple

Melt the chocolate with 1 teaspoon of the kirsch in a bowl over a pan of simmering water. Dip the strawberries in the chocolate, holding them by their stalks. Cover entirely with chocolate. Stand on silicone paper to set, then snip off the stalks.

In a bowl set over iced water, whip the cream with the sugars and the remaining kirsch until doubled in volume. Peel and core the pineapple slices. Put each slice on a plate, spoon the cream into the centres and the strawberries on top.

BURNT CREAMS
Serves Six
These are very rich. They are good served with soft fruit such as raspberries or strawberries.
½ pint/300ml double cream
½ pint/300ml single cream
4 egg yolks
1 tablespoon vanilla sugar
caster sugar

Heat the creams in a double saucepan. Mix the egg yolks and sugar and add to the creams off the heat. Return to the heat and cook until the custard coats the back of a spoon. Do not let it boil.

Pour the custard into 6 individual ramekins or soufflé dishes, filling nearly to the brim.

Stand the ramekins in a shallow baking dish. Pour in hot water to come two-thirds up the sides of the ramekins. Put the baking dish in a preheated oven at 250°F/120°C/Gas Mark ½ for 30 to 40 minutes until the custard is just set. Remove from the oven and when quite cold cover each custard with a thin even layer of caster sugar. Brown uniformly under a hot grill. Cool before serving.

TAURUS

SUN IN TAURUS 20 APRIL - 20 MAY
RULED BY VENUS

TAURUS is a fixed, cold, dry, feminine earth sign, a combination of characteristics which denote a love of tradition, the arts and all beautiful surroundings. Taureans are blessed with sound judgment, which extends to an appreciation of good food. According to the Persian astrologer Al Biruni, writing in the eleventh century, the Taurean's love of food excels that of any other sign.

TAURUS ENVIRONMENTS

Taurus is a lover of the country, and rules orchards, pastures, wheat and corn fields, barns and places where food is stored. Taureans appreciate a rural setting; a country tavern is the ideal location for a healthy farmhouse style meal. They like comfort; beautiful objects serve to excite their imagination while they eat; even a hint of decadence is often appreciated. The food, however, is usually more important than the environment. Taurus also rules cellars, so a fashionable cellar wine bar can provide an appropriate place for a celebration.

TAURUS FOODS

Taureans have a reputation for loving all kinds of food. They relish plain and simple dishes, but will never refuse rich sauces. Food from almost any country or region is served at the Taurean dinner table. In particular, Taurus rules all dairy products, artichokes, saffron, sweet fruits in general and beef. Other foods associated with this sign are those belonging to Venus, the sign's ruling planet.

SWISS CHEESE CROQUETTES
Serves Four to Six

These make an admirable lunch dish as well as a first course. If you make the croquettes small, they can also serve as hot appetizers to serve with drinks. A tomato or garlic sauce or a green pepper relish and a fresh green salad would go well with them.

2 oz/50g butter plus extra for the dish
2 oz/50g flour
½ pint/300ml milk
3 egg yolks
1 oz/25g Parmesan cheese, grated
3 oz/75g Gruyère cheese, grated
salt and pepper
nutmeg
1 beaten egg
flour or dry breadcrumbs for coating
oil for deep frying

In a saucepan, melt the butter, stir in the flour and cook for 2 minutes over a medium heat. Add the milk slowly, stirring over a gentle heat, to make a thick smooth sauce. Cook without letting the sauce burn for 8 minutes. Remove the pan from the heat and stir in the egg yolks and the cheeses. Season well.

Grease or line with clingfilm an oblong dish or baking tray. Spread the mixture over it and leave until thoroughly cool.

With floured hands, roll the mixture into balls; or shape into croquettes about 2 inches/5 cm long. Dip in the beaten egg, then in the flour or breadcrumbs. Deep fry at 350°F/175°C until golden all over.

A PERSIAN HERB OMELETTE
Serves Four

A propitious dish, served on New Year's Day in Iran — symbolizing fertility and wealth. It should be eaten cool, to keep in the cold-dry character of Taurean foods. The chopped walnuts, Venusian *par excellence*, are not always included in the recipe. Yoghurt is often served with it.

1 leek
3 oz/75g spinach

4 spring onions, tops as well
1 tablespoon chopped parsley
1 tablespoon chopped fresh coriander
1 tablespoon chopped chervil, tarragon and chives
1 tablespoon chopped walnuts
4 large eggs
salt and pepper
2 oz/50g butter

Wash, dry and chop the vegetables finely. Mix the chopped herbs with the walnuts. Beat the eggs in a bowl. Add the chopped ingredients and seasoning. Butter a flat round oven dish generously. Pour in the omelette mixture and bake in a preheated oven at 325°F/160°C/Gas Mark 3 for 45 minutes. Serve in slices when cooled.

COLD YOGHURT SOUP
Serves Four

Although the moistness of this dish goes against the character of the sign, the ingredients are so apt for both Taurus and Venus its ruler that the recipe demanded to be included.

1 cucumber
3 spring onions and their tops
2 tablespoons chopped walnuts
2 hard-boiled eggs, chopped
1 tablespoon chopped parsley
1 tablespoon chopped mint
1½ lb/700g natural yoghurt
3 tablespoons raisins
½ pint/300ml ice cold water
salt and pepper
mint leaves to garnish

Grate the cucumber coarsely. Slice the onions thinly. Add them and the chopped nuts, eggs and herbs to the yoghurt. Stir in the raisins. Add enough water to make a thick cream. Season to taste. Serve well chilled (if you like serve with ice cubes stirred in) with mint leaves to decorate.

COLD BEETROOT SOUP
Serves Four to Six

Taurus governs roots in general — thus this Russian beetroot soup, enriched by the sour cream from that other Taurean grouping, dairy foods.

The sweet apples give it a Venusian touch.
1 lb/450g small beetroot, with their tops if possible
1 slice wholemeal bread
1½ pints/900ml water
½ cucumber
2 eating apples
3 spring onions
2 hard-boiled eggs
salt and black pepper
lemon juice
5 fl oz/150ml sour cream
chopped dill to decorate

Wash the beetroot. Boil them (with some of the tops if they had them) in salted water for 30 to 45 minutes until tender. When cooked, peel and grate the beetroot into a bowl. Add the slice of bread. Bring the water to the boil and pour over. Cover and leave to stand at room temperature for 2 days. Strain and reserve the slightly fermented liquid.

Peel and finely dice or chop the cucumber, apples, onions and eggs. Add them to the liquid. Season with salt, black pepper and lemon juice. Stir in the sour cream. Decorate with dill.

VEAL ESCALOPES WITH PARMESAN CHEESE AND PARMA HAM
Serves Four
Although this way of cooking veal originates in the town of Bologna, it is the raw materials of Parma that give it its flavours. Some simple glazed carrots would go well with the syrupy Marsala sauce. Tiny new potatoes with sour cream instead of butter would also be delicious.
4 veal escalopes, each about 3-4 oz/75-125g
flour for dusting
4 oz/125g butter
4 slices Parma ham
4 oz/125g freshly grated Parmesan cheese
4 tablespoons Marsala
2 sage leaves

Dip the veal in flour. Heat half the butter in a frying pan. Add the veal and fry quickly for about a minute to brown one side. Turn the veal and while browning the other side place a slice of Parma ham and 1 ounce/25g of the Parmesan on top of each escalope. Dot with the remaining butter. Pour in the Marsala and boil fiercely for 30 seconds to reduce. Add the sage leaves to the pan. Cover and cook gently until the cheese has melted. Serve immediately.

FILLET STEAK WITH WALNUT AND HORSERADISH SAUCE
Serves Four
This makes a slight yet surprising change from the standard horseradish sauce. Serve with small buttered new potatoes and baby broad beans.
4 fillet steaks, each about 6 oz/175g and
    1 inch/2.5cm thick
salt and black pepper
1 tablespoon oil
For the sauce
2 oz/50g shelled walnuts
2 tablespoons finely grated horseradish
5 fl oz/150ml single cream
1 teaspoon sugar
salt
lemon juice

First make the sauce. Dip the walnuts in boiling water for 30 seconds. Carefully remove their skins. Chop them very finely. Mix the walnuts with the horseradish and the cream. Season with the sugar, salt and lemon juice to taste.

Trim and season the steaks. Heat the oil in a heavy frying pan until very hot. Add the steaks and fry for about 5 minutes (for rare), turning once. Rest in a warm place on a rack for 5 minutes.

Spoon the sauce onto the steaks and serve.

BEEF STUFFED WITH SALAMI AND CHEESE
Serves Four
The dish that inspired this recipe is served at the famous Charleston Restaurant in Palermo. It can be served with a salad of fennel, watercress and orange and some plain new potatoes.
2 oz/50g salami
1 hard-boiled egg

2 tablespoons chopped parsley
1 tablespoon pine kernels
2 oz/50g Emmenthal or Jarlsberg cheese, grated
1 lb/450g rumpsteak in one large slice
salt and black pepper
3 fl oz/85ml olive oil
For the tomato sauce
1 small onion
2 cloves garlic
14 oz/400g can plum tomatoes
1 teaspoon tomato purée
1 tablespoon chopped basil
salt and black pepper

Chop the salami, egg, parsley and pine kernels coarsely, and mix with the cheese. Season the meat and lay the mixture in the centre. Tie in a roll. Sear the meat in the oil in a heavy casserole. When browned, remove the meat and set aside.

To make the sauce, peel and chop the onion. Add it to the casserole and brown in the same oil. Peel and chop the garlic and add to the onion. Add the tomatoes and the purée. Mash them down. Cook fiercely for 3 minutes to reduce the liquid. Add the basil and seasoning. Place the beef roll on the sauce, cover and simmer for about 1 hour.

Carve the beef in thick slices and serve with the hot sauce poured around.

PEACHES WITH CHICKEN AND CINNAMON
Serves Four to Six
In Iran, where the combination of fruit and meat is of long tradition, the fruit comes before the meat — apt for people stirred by the passions of Venus. And, at last, a use for under-ripe peaches. Serve this soup/stew with plain rice. Almost a meal in itself, follow with goat's cheese and salad, then some sticky sweetmeats.
1 onion
4 oz/125g butter
1 chicken, about 2½ lb/1.1 kg, jointed
salt and black pepper
1 inch/2.5cm stick cinnamon, ground
1 pint/600ml water

3 under-ripe peaches
juice of 2 lemons
1 tablespoon brown sugar

Peel and chop the onion. Melt half the butter in a wide pan. Add the onion and cook gently until soft. Add the chicken joints to the pan. Raise the heat and brown all over. Add seasoning and freshly ground cinnamon. Pour in the water, cover and simmer for 25 to 30 minutes.

Peel the peaches. Cut them in sections off their stones. Melt the remaining butter in a frying pan and fry the peaches until they colour. Add them to the chicken, with lemon juice and brown sugar. Cover and simmer for a further 20 minutes. Check seasoning.

FRENCH BEANS WITH HAZELNUTS
Serves Four
Beans are under the influence of Venus. This is a delicious way of presenting the vegetable with a little more sparkle.

It is possible to make a salad with the same ingredients. Use the oils and lemon to make a dressing, adding a little Dijon mustard and single cream for taste and consistency.
12 oz/350g French beans
salt
1 oz/25g shelled hazelnuts
1 teaspoon hazelnut oil
3 teaspoons olive oil
juice of ¼ lemon
white pepper

Top, tail and string the beans. Cook in plenty of fast boiling salted water for 5 minutes or until just cooked. Drain and refresh under a cold tap.

Toast the nuts, rub off their skins and chop them.

In a saucepan heat the oils and a tablespoon of water. Add the beans and boil them fiercely to drive off the water, then toss them to ensure they are well coated with the oils. Dress with lemon juice and white pepper. Scatter with hazelnuts before serving.

TUSCAN FRIED ARTICHOKES

Serves Four as a vegetable course

Serve as an accompaniment to meat. These artichokes need no more than wedges of lemon to season them. If eaten as part of a more substantial vegetarian meal, you may wish to make a spicy tomato sauce (and increase the quantities given here).

4 oz/125g flour
3 tablespoons olive oil
1 egg, separated
6 very young globe artichokes
lemon
salt
oil for deep frying

Mix the flour, oil and yolk of egg with cold water to a smooth thin cream. Let stand for 60 minutes.

Strip each artichoke of its coarse outer leaves. Cut off the stalk and the tops. Remove the choke. Slice, as if a cake, into several thin wedges. Leave in a bowl of cold water acidulated with lemon juice (1 tablespoon of lemon juice to each pint/600 ml of water) until ready to start cooking.

Whip the egg white stiffly, fold into the batter. Season generously with salt.

Sicilian Strawberry Cream

Pat the artichoke slices dry with kitchen paper. Dip them in the batter and cook in deep oil at 375°F/190°C until golden brown. Drain on kitchen paper and serve immediately.

PERSIAN BREAD WITH CHEESE, HERBS AND SALAD
Serves Four

In many places in Iran the diner is offered a dish of fresh herbs and some flat bread to sharpen his appetite before the meal itself. Here, I have given a recipe for a thicker Persian bread and suggested you combine it with a dish of herbs, some dressed cheese and a tomato salad to make a delectable snack in the middle of the day.

Bread
1 oz/25g yeast
9 fl oz/275ml warm (90°F/32°C) water
1 lb/450g white flour
1 teaspoon salt
vegetable oil

Cream the yeast in 3 tablespoons of the water. Mix in the rest of the water. Put the flour into a mixing bowl. Make a well in the middle and pour in the yeast and water. Push a little of the flour over the surface of the water and leave to bubble for 20 minutes in a warm (75°F/25°C) place.

Add salt to the sponge mixture and mix all into a dough. Knead very well, keeping the dough moist but not sticky. Cover with a damp cloth or clingfilm and leave in a warm place for about 45 minutes, or until the dough doubles in bulk.

Oil 1 or 2 baking trays.

Divide the dough in two. Knead and shape into balls. Roll out into long ovals about ½ inch/1 cm thick. Put on the tray(s). Leave covered for 20 minutes to rise. Brush with oil and bake in the centre of a preheated oven at 425°F/220°C/Gas Mark 7 for 15 minutes until golden brown. Eat warm.

Cheese
Feta cheese, cut in slices and dressed with olive oil and freshly ground pepper would go well with this bread. An alternative would be a natural cream cheese, seasoned with pepper and a dressing sprinkled on top made from dried mint, pepper, salt and turmeric ground together.

A dish of fresh herbs
Wash and dry a selection of herbs. Break them into sprigs. Flat leaved parsley, leaf coriander, mint, chives, chervil and watercress are suitable candidates.

Tomato salad
Skin and slice large, juicy tomatoes, sun-ripened where possible, and dress them with an oily vinaigrette made with four parts olive oil to one part wine vinegar or lemon juice. Sprinkle ground cumin over the salad.

SICILIAN STRAWBERRY CREAM
Serves Four

A luscious Venusian fruit made in Sicily in a very similar way to the 'mess' of strawberries and cream served in England. Eat with almond biscuits.
1 lb/450g strawberries
½ pint/300ml double cream
5oz/150g caster sugar
juice of ½ orange

Clean the strawberries. Slice them fairly thick, reserving 6 whole strawberries for decoration. Whip the cream lightly with 4 ounces/125g of the sugar and the orange juice. Stir in the fruit quite vigorously. Pour into a bowl, sprinkle the remaining sugar over the top. Let it stand in the cool for at least 1 hour. Cut the whole strawberries into fan shapes and decorate the cream.

TANGERINE SHERBET
Serves Four

Palermo could be said to be the home of the water ice, just as Iran is the home of cooling sherbet — the chilled, but not frozen fruit syrup they take to ward off the effects of the sun. This sherbet is very sweet, so will freeze soft. Eat it with almond biscuits. In the Middle East they also make jam with the juice and peel of the tangerine, sometimes serving it as a sweet, with whipped cream.

zest of 2 tangerines
juice of 12 tangerines, enough to make
  1 pint/600ml
7 oz/200g icing sugar
2 tablespoons Mandarine Napoleon liqueur
1 pink grapefruit

Grate the zest of 2 tangerines. Dissolve the sugar in the tangerine juice. Add the liqueur and zest. Pour the mixture into a container, cover tightly and put in the freezer. No beating is required as the mixture is so sweet. Or use an ice cream maker. Serve very soon after freezing.

Take the peel and pith off the grapefruit. Section it, removing all skin and core. Arrange sections round the tangerine sherbet on plates and serve.

CARAMEL WALNUTS STUFFED WITH MARZIPAN
Makes twelve

Walnuts and almonds, fruits of Venus, in a sweetmeat from Iran, is a luxurious way to finish your meal. Uncooked marzipan, equal quantities of ground almonds and sugar, with some flavouring, is a long established Persian sweetmeat — going by the charming name of *Toot*.

3 oz/75g ground almonds
3 oz/75g icing sugar
2-3 tablespoons orange flower water
12 shelled walnuts
oil
3 oz/75g brown sugar

Mix the ground almonds and icing sugar. Add the orange water and make a paste. Sandwich the walnut halves with the *toot*. Leave on an oiled tray. Put the brown sugar in a pan and heat, while stirring, to caramelize. Pour a little on each walnut sandwich and leave to cool.

STEAMED MARMALADE PUDDING
Serves Four

This light steamed pudding is quintessential Scotland cooked in a Lunar mode — with lots of water. Serve the pudding with a custard as well as the hot marmalade.

4 oz/125g butter plus extra for the pudding bowl
4 oz/125g caster sugar
4 oz/125g self-raising flour
2 eggs, weighing approx. 4 oz/125g
6 oz/175g good orange marmalade

Cream the butter in a bowl. Add the sugar, beating all the while. Add a tablespoon of flour and an egg alternately, beating hard. Fold in the rest of the flour and half the marmalade. Mix thoroughly. Pour into a greased 2 pint/1.1 litre pudding bowl. Cover with greaseproof paper and tie down with string. Steam for about 2 hours.

Melt the rest of the marmalade with 2 fluid ounces/60 ml water. Turn the pudding onto a dish and pour the marmalade over the top.

CINNAMON APPLE CRUMBLE
Serves Four

This is inspired by an Irish dish called Friar's Omelette. Serve it with whipped cream.

1 lb/450g cooking apples
2 oz/50g brown sugar
2 cloves
2 oz/50g butter, plus extra for the dish
juice of ½ lemon
2 eggs, beaten
For the topping
4 oz/125g soft breadcrumbs
1 teaspoon ground cinnamon
1 oz/25g brown sugar
2 oz/50g butter

Peel, core and quarter the apples. Put the apples in a saucepan with 2 tablespoons of water, the sugar and the heads of the cloves. Stir to dissolve the sugar then cook to a purée. Mix in the butter and lemon juice until absorbed. Leave to cool. Mix in the beaten eggs.

Butter an ovenproof dish and pour in the apple mixture.

Make the topping by mixing the breadcrumbs, cinnamon and sugar. Spread over the apple mixture. Dot with the butter. Cook in a preheated oven at 375°F/190°C/Gas Mark 5 for 20 to 30 minutes. Serve warm or cool.

GEMINI

SUN IN GEMINI 21 MAY - 20 JUNE
RULED BY MERCURY

GEMINI is the sign of communication and travel and Geminians tend to be lively, talkative and interested in just about anything. Sometimes, however, they incline strongly towards literary subjects, considering too great an interest in food as beneath them. Some may even prefer to read or talk about food than actually cook it. Those who do develop a close interest in food experiment widely with dishes from other cultures, and they are likely to collect recipe books, or even to compile their own. Gemini is a hot, moist, masculine air sign.

GEMINI ENVIRONMENTS
Gemini rules hills and mountains, forests and fields used for hunting, river banks, gambling resorts, palaces and musicians' houses. Ideal locations for Geminian meals include mountain inns, casinos, stately homes and river-side hostelries, with music providing the perfect background. Talkative guests and witty after dinner conversation complete the meal, although the solitary Gemini will make up for the lack of company by reading or watching TV while eating. When eating out the Geminian shows interest in guests at adjacent tables and, if by a window, enjoys watching the passers-by. As a sign of travel, Gemini also rules station buffets and any vehicle on which food is served.

GEMINI FOOD
As an impatient and versatile sign, Gemini is associated with all dishes that take minimum time to prepare and eat. It is also associated with a mixture of dishes and tastes. The modern fast food industry is typically Geminian, especially food that can be eaten while walking down the street or on the move. The foods specifically ruled by this sign are domestic fowls, mainly chicken and turkey. Vegetables include fennel, sorrel and turnip; and flavourings include aniseed, camomile and hyssop. Other foods associated with Gemini are those ruled by Mercury, the sign's ruling planet.

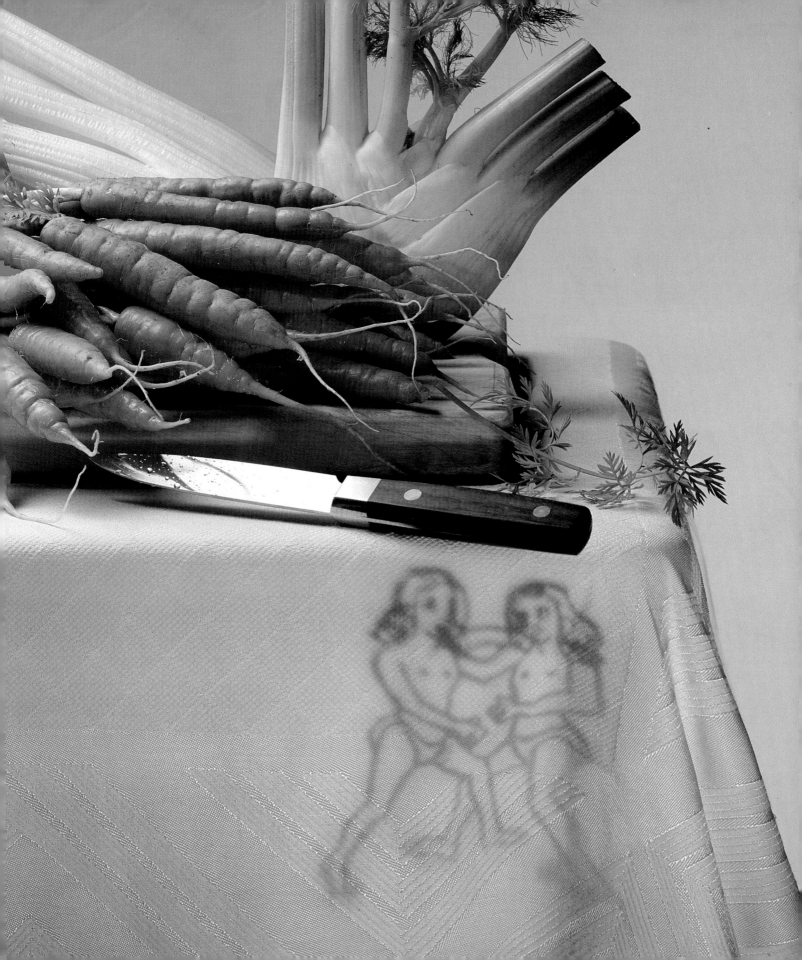

CARROT AND CORIANDER SOUP
Serves Six
You can make this creamy soup more substantial by frying sippets of bread in butter to accompany it.
4 oz/125g onions
1 lb/450g carrots
2 oz/50g butter
1 tablespoon finely ground coriander
2 pints/1.1 litres chicken stock
salt and black pepper
5 fl oz/150ml double cream

Peel and slice the onions and carrots. Melt the butter in a saucepan. Add the vegetables, cover the pan and cook for 20 minutes. Stir in the coriander. Add the stock and seasoning and simmer for 15 minutes. Blend until smooth or put through the fine plate of a food mill. Return the soup to the heat and stir in the cream. Check seasoning.

SISTER ABIGAIL'S BLUE FLOWER OMELETTE
Serves One
Who has not had their little patch of chives go to flower before the onion-flavoured stalks have all been cut? This is a way of using the blooms, according to an American Shaker recipe (the sister in the title). To make it an all-American main course serve with Hashed Browns (*see* page 32).

For each omelette
2 eggs
2 tablespoons milk
salt and black pepper
6 chive flowers
butter

Beat the eggs, milk and seasoning with a fork in a small bowl. Stir in the flowers.

Melt a small knob of butter over medium high heat in an 8 inch/20 cm omelette pan until hot but not quite smoking. Pour the omelette mixture into the pan to cover the bottom. Stir the mixture with the back of the fork for 20 seconds. Turn down the heat to medium. Pull back the edges of the omelette to allow the uncooked runny mixture to come in contact with the heat. When it is sufficiently cooked, and an omelette should still be creamy inside — not entirely set — fold it in half and tip out of the pan onto a warmed plate.

Repeat the process as often as required for the number of diners, wiping out and rebuttering the pan each time.

FENNEL AND MIMOSA SALAD
Serves Four
More flowers for Gemini, in a salad that is eaten in Tunisia and Egypt. But you can make it at home with mimosa from the florist. The flavour of bulb fennel is often well balanced by something acid like orange or green olives, which could be served with this salad to extend it, along with some herbed cream cheese. The salad is also very refreshing after a rich meat dish.
2 bulbs fennel
2 teaspoons walnut oil
3 tablespoons olive oil
1 tablespoon white wine vinegar
salt and black pepper
1 branch flowering mimosa

Take off any coarse outer layers of the fennel. Slice very thinly. Make a dressing of the oils, vinegar and salt and black pepper. Toss the fennel in this and leave for 2 hours. Strip the blossoms from the mimosa and scatter over the salad before serving.

CELERIAC REMOULADE
Serves Four
Serve this salad with small slices of bread fried in olive oil.
1 small celeriac
5 fl oz/150ml thick lemon mayonnaise
2 fl oz/50ml single cream
5 teaspoons Dijon mustard (or more to taste)
salt and black pepper
wine vinegar
parsley sprigs

Peel the celeriac and cut into fine matchsticks.

Drop into acidulated water (1 tablespoon lemon juice or vinegar to each pint/600 ml of water) and leave until you are ready to use.

Drain the celeriac and blanch in boiling salted water for 30 seconds. Drain, refresh under a cold tap and dry well.

Mix the mayonnaise and single cream. Add the mustard and season well, adding vinegar if necessary. Mix with the celeriac. Decorate with the parsley sprigs.

SMOKED SALMON AND CAVIAR ROLLS
Serves Four

These filled rolls are inspired by the cooking of San Francisco and Los Angeles. There, they are cooked as pizzas but the luscious flavours and textures enclosed within these rolls make them grenades of temptation. They are quite rich, so a first course needs to be light, a clear soup or a Greek *avgolemono* perhaps, and a plate of mixed spring vegetables to accompany them.

8 white bread rolls
8 oz/225g butter
1 sweet onion
10 fl oz/300ml sour cream
1 small bunch dill, chopped
black pepper
12 oz/350g smoked salmon pieces
lemon juice, optional
4 teaspoons caviar

Cut the tops off the rolls and reserve. Carefully hollow out the crumb without breaking through the crust. Melt 7 ounces/200g of the butter and brush the tops and rolls with it. Bake them in a preheated oven 400°F/200°C/Gas Mark 6 for 5 to 10 minutes until golden.

Peel and chop the onion. Cook it in the rest of the butter. When the onion is soft, stir in the sour cream, dill and black pepper. Cook until amalgamated and thick. Add the smoked salmon pieces and warm through. Taste for seasoning, adding lemon juice if desired. Fill the rolls with the smoked salmon mixture, put ½ teaspoon of caviar on each, replace their tops and serve.

RED MULLET WITH PIMENTOS
Serves Four

Serve it with some sippets of fried bread and wedges of lemon.

4 red mullet, each about 8 oz/225g before gutting
1 onion
3 fl oz/85ml olive oil
2 tablespoons chopped parsley
salt and black pepper
2 cloves garlic
3 canned red peppers
paprika

Gut the fish, leave their heads on and their livers in. Peel and slice half the onion. Put 1 tablespoon of the olive oil in a casserole and fry the sliced onion for about 3 minutes until translucent. Add 1 tablespoon of the chopped parsley and 2 tablespoons water. Put the fish on top, season with salt and pepper. Cover very tightly and cook in a cool oven, preheated to 250°F/120°C/Gas Mark ½, for 20 to 30 minutes until the fish is tender.

Take the fish out, put on a dish and keep warm.

Strain the cooking liquor. Chop the other half of the onion roughly and peel the garlic. Put the onion, garlic, peppers and the rest of the parsley in a blender with the cooking liquor. Blend to a purée. Pour the remaining oil in a thin stream into the blender and continue processing. Pour the puréed sauce into a saucepan and reheat, tasting for seasoning. Pour the sauce round the fish, dust with paprika and serve.

CORN AND MARIGOLD PUDDING
Serves Four

Another flower recipe from the United States. You can use dried marigold petals from herbalists. If picking from the garden, take the blooms from your pot marigolds, not the French ones. Serve with a dish of peas and lettuce.

2 oz/50g butter plus extra for the dish
2 eggs
1 lb/450g canned creamed sweetcorn
salt
cayenne pepper

5 fl oz/150ml milk
5 fl oz/150ml single cream
6 marigold flowers
4 oz/125g cooked ham
2 oz/50g grated Parmesan cheese

Grease a 2 pint/1.1 litre soufflé dish.

Separate the eggs. Melt the butter. Put the sweetcorn in a bowl and beat in the egg yolks. Add the butter, seasoning, milk and cream. (If your sweetcorn is not creamed, put all this through the blender.)

Strip the petals off the marigolds and cut the ham in strips. Stir both into the sweetcorn mixture.

Breast of Turkey with Four Spices

Beat the egg whites to firm peaks and fold in. Pour the mixture into the soufflé dish. Sprinkle the cheese over the top.

Stand the soufflé dish in a baking tin. Pour in enough hot water to come two-thirds up the sides of the dish. Put the baking dish in a preheated oven at 350°F/180°C/Gas Mark 4 for 45 to 60 minutes.

BREAST OF TURKEY WITH FOUR SPICES
Serves Four
Though spices are ruled by Mars or Jupiter in the main, their combination in this dish, each setting off the other yet never seeming 'curried', may take

on some of the characteristics of Mercury with the planet's affinity with flavour enhancers. Serve with a slightly enriched pilaff and a purée of parsnip.

1 turkey breast, sufficient for 6 oz/175g of meat per person
1 tablespoon coriander seeds
12 cardamom pods
½ teaspoon cloves
1 oz/25g fresh ginger root
1 tablespoon olive oil
salt and pepper
1 large onion
2 oz/50g butter
2 fl oz/50ml white wine
5 fl oz/150ml double cream
lemon juice

Skin and bone the turkey and cut into 4 escalopes. Using a spice grinder, grind the coriander, the seeds from the cardamom pods and the heads of the cloves finely; peel and grate the ginger. Mix all the spices into a paste with the oil, seasoning with salt and pepper. Spread this paste over the escalopes and leave, covered, in the refrigerator for 2 hours or more.

Peel and chop the onion. Heat the butter in a large ovenproof pan and fry the onion gently until tender. Increase the heat to high and add the turkey escalopes. Turn the escalopes over then add the white wine, bring to the boil and place, covered, in a preheated oven at 275°F/140°C/Gas Mark 1. Cook for about 10 minutes or until they are done.

Remove the escalopes to a serving dish and keep warm. Add the double cream to the pan and boil to reduce to a thickish consistency. Taste for seasoning, it may need lemon juice to sharpen it. Pour over the turkey and serve.

HASHED BROWNS
Serves Four
Because the culinary character of Gemini is defined as hot-wet, these hashed browns are made from boiled potatoes, not raw ones.

1½ lb/700g boiled potatoes
4 oz/125g salt pork fat or bacon fat
pepper and salt

Cut the potatoes into small cubes. It is best if they are still quite firm. Melt the fat in a heavy pan. Add the potatoes and pepper and salt, taking into account the saltiness of the fat. Stir the potatoes over a high heat for 3 minutes. Then leave to cook over a medium heat until well browned underneath. Invert onto a hot dish.

SAN FRANCISCO SOURDOUGH BREAD
Makes two large loaves
Although Gemini foods are fast, light and changeable, they have to be eaten with *something*. This bread, for which San Francisco is famous, would do for any sort of meal. The sourdough technique is long-winded, and the American system is not the same as the European. But try it for bread with a difference.

Starter
4 fl oz/120ml milk
4 fl oz/120ml water
4 oz/125g strong wholemeal flour
1 teaspoon sugar
¼ teaspoon salt
¼ oz/7g fresh yeast

Sponge
the starter
1 lb/450g strong unbleached white flour
8 fl oz/250ml water (at 100°F/38°C)
1 teaspoon salt
1 teaspoon sugar

Dough
½ oz/15g fresh yeast
2 fl oz/50ml water (at 100°F/38°C)
the sponge
6-10oz/175-275g strong unbleached white flour
oil for the baking sheets

To make the starter, scald the milk and mix with the water. Beat in the flour, sugar and salt. Leave in a bowl covered with a cloth for 3 days at

80°F/27°C. Crumble, then beat the yeast into the mixture. Leave for another 3 days, stirring daily. Refrigerate.

To make the sponge, mix the starter with the rest of the ingredients and stir well. Cover and leave for 6 hours at 80°F/27°C, until doubled in bulk.

To make the dough, dissolve the yeast in the water. Add to the sponge. Knead in as much of the flour as makes a stiff dough. Knead well. Leave covered at 80°F/27°C for 2 hours or until doubled in size. Punch down, leave to rise for 45 minutes, until size is regained.

Grease 2 baking sheets.

Divide the dough into two. Make 2 long loaves and place on the baking sheets. Put to rise at 85°F/30°C, covered with oiled clingfilm, for at least an hour, until well risen.

Preheat the oven to 425°F/220°C/Gas Mark 7. Slash the loaves with 3 diagonal cuts and place at the top of the oven. Using a laundry or plant sprayer, mist with a fine spray of water for the first 5 minutes of cooking. After another 10 minutes turn the oven down to 375°F/190°C/Gas Mark 5.

After another 20 minutes (35 minutes all told) test for cooking. The loaves should sound hollow when tapped. Leave to cook for another 10 minutes if not ready. Cool completely on racks before slicing.

DEEP FRIED CAULIFLOWER
Serves Four

An Egyptian way of cooking cauliflower, also found throughout the Mediterranean world. Egyptians often stew the fried vegetable some more on top of a tomato sauce. Alternatives are a sauce made with *tahini* — sesame seed paste — or with anchovies, garlic and onion.

1 cauliflower
2 eggs
salt and black pepper
flour
oil for deep frying
tomato sauce as in Beef Stuffed with Salami and
   Cheese on page 23, optional

Wash and strip the cauliflower, break into florets. Blanch in salted water for 5 minutes. Drain well. In a shallow dish beat the eggs lightly with salt and black pepper. Dip the florets in the egg and then roll in the flour. Deep fry in hot oil at 375°F/190°C until golden, turning as necessary. Drain on kitchen paper. Serve immediately.

If you wish to keep to the Egyptian ideal, place the cauliflower on the tomato sauce in a casserole and simmer for 20 minutes until utterly tender.

ONION BREAD RING
Serves Four

A speciality of Lombardy, this simple ring pizza makes a dish you can cut into small slices as an appetizer, or serve hot for a bolstering meal without meat. If the latter, make a tomato salad with cheese and black olives to go with it.

½ oz/15g fresh yeast
5 fl oz/50ml water (at 100°F/38°C)
9 oz/250g plain flour
2 fl oz/50 ml olive oil plus extra for the baking sheet
1 teaspoon salt
1½ lb/700g red onions
4 oz/125g butter
salt and black pepper

Dissolve the yeast in the water. Put the flour in a mixing bowl. Make a well in the centre and pour in the yeast and water. Add the oil and salt. Mix then knead very well to make a moist but not sticky dough. Put to rise covered with clingfilm in a warm place at 80°F/27°C for 45 minutes, until doubled in bulk.

Knead the dough again and form into a long roll. Turn this into a ring, pinching the ends of the roll together. Grease a baking sheet and put the dough ring on it, cover with greased clingfilm, and leave to rise at 80°F/27°C for 45 minutes.

Meanwhile, peel and slice the onions. Fry them gently, without colouring, in the butter until they are soft. Season with salt and pepper and remove from the heat. When slightly cooled, pile them onto the dough ring. Bake in a preheated oven at 425°F/220°C/Gas Mark 7 for 15 minutes. Reduce the heat to 350°F/180°C/Gas Mark 4 and bake for a further 10 minutes.

Put the breadring on a rack immediately to save the bottom from going soggy. Eat hot or cold.

VIOLET PUDDING
Serves Four

More flowers for the sign of the Twins — from Wales, where the recipe was gathered by Bobby Freeman from a diary of a farmer's wife for 1796. Quite delicious, and very simple.

butter for greasing the dish
5 oz/150g dried violets, from a herbalist
6 eggs
1 tablespoon honey
juice of 1 lemon
cream for serving

Butter a small baking dish.

Simmer the violets in a little water for 2 to 3 minutes and drain.

Beat the eggs with the honey and lemon. Stir in the violets and pour into the baking dish. Stand the dish in a shallow baking tin. Pour in enough hot water to come two-thirds up the sides of the dish. Put the baking tin in a preheated oven at 250°F/130°C/Gas Mark ½ for about 45 minutes until set. Serve with cream.

SPICED RICE PUDDING AND AN ORANGE FLOWER AND ROSE CONSERVE
Serves Four

A combination of the spices of the Far East and the flowers of the New World. The sweet conserve is a recipe from the American South and makes this an arresting dessert.

1 tablespoon pudding rice
1 pint/600ml milk
1 oz/25g sugar
2 cardamom pods
1 stick cinnamon

For the conserve
2 oz/50g dried orange flower petals, from a herbalist
2 tablespoons water
1½ lbs/700g caster sugar
8 fl oz/250ml rose water (not concentrated)

Put the rice, milk, sugar and spices in a double boiler. Stir to dissolve the sugar. Cook, covered, for 1½ to 2½ hours, until the rice is tender. Remove the spices.

To make the conserve, crush the orange flower petals to a powder in a mortar. Soak them in the water. Add the sugar and stir to dissolve over a low heat.

Add the rose water and cook to a thick syrup for at least 20 minutes. It will not set entirely. Pot in glass jars, for you will not need all of this for the rice pudding. Serve cold or lukewarm.

APPLE FOOL WITH GINGER
Serves Four

The Mercurial nature of Gemini is seen in the way that one flavour sets off another. Here, the ginger accents and draws out the taste of the apple.

2 lb/900g eating apples
4 oz/125g granulated sugar
2 tablespoons preserved ginger syrup
3 knobs preserved ginger, chopped
10 fl oz/300ml double cream
1 oz/25g icing sugar

Peel, core and roughly slice the apples. Put them in a saucepan with 3 tablespoons water and the granulated sugar. Stir to dissolve the sugar and cook to a purée. Set aside to cool.

Stir in the ginger syrup and chopped ginger. Whip the cream. Fold half into the apple. Taste for sweetness.

Spoon the fool into glasses. Mix the rest of the cream with the icing sugar and put on top.

CANCER

SUN IN CANCER 21 JUNE - 22 JULY
RULED BY THE MOON

CANCER is the sign of the archetypal mother, and so of the home-maker. Cancer types are required to provide emotional support for their families, and to cook meals which are at the same time lavish and wholesome. In the contemporary world most people have to go out to work and the traditional Cancerian domestic role has been played down. However, given emotional and financial security and sufficient spare time the true Cancerian will devote much care and attention to the culinary arts. Cancer is a cold, moist, watery, fertile, feminine sign, and rules the digestive system in general.

CANCER ENVIRONMENTS

All places near water are ruled by Cancer. Cancers enjoy eating at riverside bars, lakeshore restaurants or on pleasure cruisers. In general, however, the main requirement for any public meal is peace and quiet. Cancers love a classic romantic setting, whether watching the sun set over the sea, or dining in a secluded candlelit corner of a delightful old restaurant. As lovers of tradition they prefer the old to the modern, but wealth holds little fascination for them and they would as soon eat in a simple café as in the smartest hotel. What is important to them is character and charm, and stimulation for their romantic imaginations.

CANCER FOODS

Cancer rules rice, cane sugar, cabbage, turnip, comfrey, sage and watercress. Through its connections with water it also rules all shellfish including crabs, lobsters, cockles, mussels and oysters as well as frogs and snails. Other foods associated with this sign are those ruled by the Moon. Breast meat is Cancerian.

SALAD OF COURGETTES AND MINT, WITH EGGS
Serves Four

A very simple first course from North Africa. If you wish to elaborate it, you could serve some of the dishes from the Meze on page 54, and pitta bread.

1 lb/450g very young courgettes
salt
3 tablespoons olive oil
2 teaspoons lemon juice
½ teaspoon *harissa* — N. African chilli paste
2 tablespoons chopped mint
2 tablespoons pine kernels
4 hard-boiled eggs

Wipe, top and tail and slice the courgettes very thinly. In a large saucepan blanch them for 30 seconds in briskly boiling salted water. Drain well.

Toss the courgettes in the oil immediately. Add the lemon juice, *harissa*, chopped mint, pine kernels and a pinch of salt. Toss again. Peel and quarter the eggs. Arrange them around the courgettes on a dish.

CRAB BISQUE
Serves Six

The sign of Cancer has to have a crab dish although it governs shellfish in general. The nature of the foods of the sign and of its ruler, the Moon, is that they should be wet. Hence this ultra-luxurious crab soup is most apt.

1 boiled hen crab, about 2-3 lb/900g-1.4kg
1 large onion
1 large carrot
2 sticks celery
2 oz/50g butter
bouquet garni of bay leaf, parsley stalks, thyme and
    fennel
4 tablespoons brandy
1 oz/25g flour
4 large tomatoes, Marmande or any cooking
    variety, chopped
1 pint/600ml fish stock
½ bottle dry white wine

juice of ½ lemon
salt
cayenne pepper
4 tablespoons double cream
1 tablespoon chopped parsley

Pick the crab: save the legs, shell and brown meat; reserve the white meat; discard the sac and gills. Prepare and coarsely slice the onion, carrot and celery.

Melt the butter in a saucepan and fry the vegetables and herbs. Break up the legs and shell with a hammer or rolling pin and add to the pan along with the brown meat. Fry for 5 minutes over a high heat.

In a ladle or small pan, warm the brandy. Set it alight and pour immediately over the crab and vegetables. When the flames subside lower the heat to medium. Stir in the flour and cook for a minute. Add the tomatoes. Gradually add the fish stock, white wine and lemon juice. Stir well to make sure there are no lumps. Season with salt and cayenne. Cover and simmer for 2 hours over the lowest heat possible.

Strain the soup discarding the shells and vegetables. Season to taste with salt and cayenne.

To serve, heat the white meat gently in the soup. Pour into bowls and stir in a little cream.

SALAD OF MIXED SHELLFISH WITH TOMATO AND ONION
Serves Four

Continental Africa is fond of the chilli as a flavouring and many of their best dishes include it in some form or another. There is a wealth of shellfish around the coast. This salad uses some of them, with species that are more readily available in northern countries. The giant prawns now imported from East Africa are here replaced by large frozen *crevettes roses*, available in most good fishmongers. Serve the salad with a home made mayonnaise.

For the crevettes roses
1 small onion
½ fresh chilli, seeded

1 inch/2.5cm piece fresh ginger root
2 tablespoons groundnut oil
juice of ¼ lemon
salt
4-8 frozen *crevettes roses*, defrosted and shelled
For the other shellfish
8 oysters
12 mussels
4 clams
4 scallops
1 onion
2 large tomatoes
1 tablespoon groundnut oil
juice of 2 lemons
salt
pinch of chilli powder *or* ¼ dried chilli,
   chopped
cos lettuce
lambs' leaves/corn salad
12 radishes

To cook the crevettes roses
Peel and chop the onion very fine; chop the chilli; peel and chop the ginger. Heat the oil in a saucepan. Add the onion and cook gently until soft. Add the chilli and ginger, lemon juice and salt. Add the *crevettes roses* and toss them briefly to mix. Leave to cool.

To cook the other shellfish
Clean the oysters, mussels and clams. Put them in a pot with a tablespoon of water. Cover and cook over high heat until the shells have opened. Remove the flesh from shells. Strain and reserve the liquor. Slice the scallops in three horizontally.

Peel and chop the onion very fine; skin, seed and chop the tomatoes to a pulp. Put the onion and tomatoes in a bowl and stir in the oil, lemon juice, salt and chilli. Mix in the shellfish. Leave in the refrigerator for 2 hours. The scallops will 'cook' in the lemon juice.

Wash and dry the lettuce and corn salad. Slice the radishes. Moisten the shellfish mixture, if necessary, with 1 tablespoon of the reserved liquor.

Arrange the salad leaves and radishes on a large dish. Put the shellfish and *crevette rose* on top and serve.

SQUID VENEZIANA, STEWED IN ITS OWN INK
Serves Four

Venice — Lunar city of lagoons — is the inspiration for this simple stew of the youngest squid, or cuttlefish, you can buy. If you can only get larger fish, they will need slicing and longer cooking. Very good Californian small squid are often available frozen. Venetians eat stewed squid with a dish of *polenta* (boiled corn meal). Mashed potato could be a northern substitute, with sippets of fried bread dipped in chopped parsley.

The squid can be cooked one day and reheated and eaten the next.

1½-2 lb/700-900g squid
1 onion
2 cloves garlic
5 fl oz/150ml olive oil
salt and black pepper
5 fl oz/150ml red wine

Clean and wash the squid, leaving the bodies whole unless they are very large. Reserve the small ink sacs from the innards.

Peel and slice the onion and garlic. In a casserole, cook them gently in the olive oil. Add the squid, salt and pepper. Stew gently for 20 minutes. Add the wine and the ink from the sacs. Stew for a further 5 minutes. Check the seasoning and that the squid is tender. If it seems to need much more cooking, the casserole may be left in a preheated cool oven at 225°F/110°C/Gas Mark ¼ for as long as necessary.

BREAST OF CHICKEN WITH CUCUMBER
Serves Four

The Moon, ruler of Cancer, is the planet of mothers and babies. The breast of chicken is chosen purposely therefore; and poaching is the preferred mode of cooking for Lunar foods are moist — just as cucumber is a Lunar vegetable. Serve this dish with creamed potato, and follow it with some spinach.

1 stick celery
approx. ½ pint/300ml good chicken stock

4 chicken breasts
1 cucumber
1 oz/25g butter
5 fl oz/150ml dry white wine
salt and black pepper
a pinch ground mace
2 egg yolks
2 tablespoons single cream
chopped parsley for serving

Slice the celery thinly. Put it in a pan with the stock and bring to the boil. Add the chicken breasts, cover the pan and simmer gently for about 20 minutes until they are cooked. Remove the skins and keep the chicken warm. Strain and reserve the stock.

Peel, seed and cut the cucumber into batons. In a sauté pan melt the butter and lightly brown the cucumber. Add the white wine and an equal amount of the reserved stock. Add salt, pepper and a pinch of mace. Simmer until just cooked, about 5 minutes.

Mix the egg yolks with the cream in a small bowl. Stir in 3 or 4 spoonfuls of the hot stock then gradually add the mixture to the cucumber and stock, off the heat. Return to the heat and cook gently until thickened, stirring all the while. Do not allow the sauce to boil.

Serve the breasts of chicken on top of the sauce, generously sprinkled with chopped parsley.

HADDOCK WITH MANGOES AND COCONUT
Serves Four
Lunar vegetables are both succulent, watery and, often, unripe. So the use of unripe mangoes in this dish, inspired by a Dutch way with haddock, or any other white fish, is particularly apt as well as delicious. In Holland, they make a sauce based on mango chutney. Offer boiled rice and follow it with a gratin of pumpkin.
1 large onion
2 unripe mangoes
knob of fresh ginger root
2 oz/50g butter

4 haddock fillets with skins, weighing 2 lb/900g
4 fl oz/120ml white wine
salt and black pepper
3 oz/75g creamed coconut
6 fl oz/175ml hot water
lemon
chopped fresh coriander for decoration

Peel and slice the onion thinly; peel the mangoes and slice them thinly off their stones; peel and grate the ginger.

Put the onion with the butter in an oval flame-proof oven dish and fry without colouring over a gentle flame. Add the haddock, mangoes, ginger and white wine. Season with salt and pepper. Bring to the boil then cook, covered, in a cool oven at 225°F/110°C/Gas Mark ¼ for about 15 minutes until tender. Remove the fish to a warm dish.

Dissolve the creamed coconut in the water with a pinch of salt. Add to the mangoes and cooking liquid. Cook very gently until the sauce has thickened. (Too rapid a cooking will cause it to curdle.) Taste for seasoning, add lemon juice if desired. Pour the sauce round the fish. Decorate with chopped coriander.

TAGINE OF CHICKEN WITH APPLES
Serves Four to Six
This is a Moroccan *tagine*, cooked long and slowly so that the meat is melting and the sweet spices meld with the apples put in at the end of cooking. Serve it with *couscous* and two salads — one of leaves, the other of black olives and orange dressed with ground coriander, cumin and chilli. Or the Orange Salad with Cinnamon on page 42 would serve equally well.
1 chicken
2 large onions
1 bunch parsley
3 oz/75g butter
1 pinch saffron
1 tablespoon honey
½ teaspoon ground ginger
½ teaspoon ground cinnamon
salt and black pepper

Salad of Mixed Shellfish with Tomato and Onion

4 large eating apples
2 oz/50g blanched almonds
vegetable oil
2 teaspoons sesame seeds

Joint the chicken; peel and chop the onions finely; chop the parsley. Combine all the ingredients except the apples, nuts, oil and sesame seeds in a casserole with water to barely cover. Bring to the boil and simmer very slowly for about 35 to 40 minutes or until just tender.

Peel, core and slice the apples and add to the pot. Cook for about 5 minutes until the apples are tender but not broken up.

Fry the almonds in a little oil. Toast the sesame seeds in the oven.

Serve the *tagine* in a dish, decorate with the almonds and sprinkle with the sesame seeds.

STUFFED MUSHROOMS, POLISH STYLE
Serves Four
If you increase the quantities, this would make an excellent supper dish, served perhaps with boiled potatoes. Otherwise, it goes well with roast or grilled meats.

8 large mushrooms
4 oz/125g button mushrooms
2 oz/50g onion
1 oz/25g butter plus extra for the dish
1 egg, beaten
2 tablespoons sour cream
lemon juice
salt and pepper
2 tablespoons white wine
chopped dill

Peel or wipe the large mushrooms; remove and chop their stalks; wipe and chop the button mushrooms; peel and chop the onion. Fry the onion in the butter over a medium heat. Add the chopped mushrooms and fry for a minute or two. Increase the heat to high and cook for 3 to 4 minutes, boiling away some of the liquid.

Mix in the egg, sour cream and a squeeze of lemon juice. Season to taste. Spread the mixture on the large mushrooms. Put in a greased baking dish with the white wine. Bake at the top of a preheated oven at 425°F/220°C/Gas Mark 7 for 15 to 20 minutes. Serve with a sprinkling of chopped dill.

POTATOES WITH MINT AND GARLIC
Serves at least Four
Mint always seems a Lunar herb, though rosemary and hyssop are the two most frequently connected with the planet. The Algerians often make this a more substantial dish stirring in beaten eggs at the end of cooking — a sort of Spanish omelette.
2 lb/900g new potatoes
6 cloves garlic
3 tablespoons olive oil
salt and black pepper
paprika
1 small bunch mint, chopped

Peel and dice the potatoes. Peel and crush the garlic and cook very gently, without colouring, in the oil. Add salt, pepper and paprika. Add the potatoes to the garlic and barely cover with water. Cook gently until just done. Stir the mint into the potatoes and serve.

A SALAD OF AVOCADO AND CUCUMBER
Serves Four
The foods of the Moon are ideally cold and uncooked. It may not be easy to compose a meal on these lines, unless at high summer. But this is the reason for the large number of salads in this vegetable section.
½ cucumber
salt
small bunch dill
2 tablespoons double cream
1 teaspoon vinegar
black pepper
2 avocados
2 bunches watercress

Grate the cucumber. Leave it sprinkled with some salt to drain in a colander under a lightly weighted saucer. Rinse and pat dry with kitchen paper.

Chop the dill. Mix the cucumber, dill, cream and vinegar in a bowl. Season to taste.

Halve the avocados, remove the stones. Peel them and cut each half into thin slices. Fan the slices out on plates with the cucumber sauce at the apex of the fan. Serve with washed watercress.

ORANGE SALAD WITH CINNAMON
Serves Four
3 oranges
1 tablespoon rosewater
½ teaspoon ground cinnamon

Peel and section the oranges, avoiding all pith. Put them in a serving bowl, sprinkle with rosewater and dust with cinnamon.

MELON SORBET WITH PEACHES
Serves Four
The success of the sorbet depends on having a very ripe (even overripe) flavourful melon. The amount of lemon juice (and sugar) will depend on the ripeness of the fruits.
7 oz/200g plus 1 tablespoon caster sugar
8 fl oz/250ml water
10 fl oz/300ml melon purée

lemon juice
4 ripe peaches
8 oz/225g loganberries

Dissolve 4 ounces/125g of the sugar in the water over low heat. Then boil for 3 minutes. When the syrup is cool add to the melon purée, season if necessary with lemon juice. Freeze in an ice cream maker

Peel the peaches by dipping them in boiling water. Cut into thin sections off the stone. Sprinkle with 1 tablespoon sugar and some lemon juice. Blend the loganberries with the remaining sugar. Add some lemon juice if necessary. Press through a fine sieve.

On very cold plates put pools of loganberry sauce. Arrange fans of peaches on top. Give each person a spoonful of sorbet at the centre of the peach fan.

ATHOLL BROSE
Serves Four
A Scottish recipe. More exactly, when the mixture is for eating, not drinking, it should be called Gromach, but the other name has now stuck. It can be served with a bowl of fresh raspberries.
2 oz/50g coarse 'pinhead' oatmeal
15 fl oz/450ml double cream
2 tablespoons heather honey
2 tablespoons Scotch malt whisky

Toast the oatmeal in a heavy pan in a preheated oven at 350°F/180°C/Gas Mark 4 for 10 minutes until lightly browned.

In a bowl whip the cream until stiff. Fold in the honey, whisky and oatmeal. Spoon into syllabub glasses. Leave for 1 hour before serving.

STRAWBERRIES AND REDCURRANTS
Serves Four
1 lb/450g redcurrants
2 fl oz/60ml water
approx. 12 oz/350g caster sugar
1 lb/450g strawberries
5 fl oz/150ml double cream
1 teaspoon icing sugar

In a saucepan cook the redcurrants with the water until soft. Strain off the juice, pressing to extract as much as possible.

Measure the juice and return to the pan. Add 1 pound/450g of caster sugar to each pint/600 ml of juice or pro rata. Stir to dissolve the sugar, then boil for 4 minutes.

Put the strawberries in a large bowl and pour the hot syrup over them. Strain the syrup back into the pan and reboil for 1 minute. Pour once again over the strawberries. Repeat for a third time. Now leave the syrup to cool with the strawberries. In this way the strawberries will be softened but retain their fresh taste.

Serve with stiffly whipped cream sweetened with the icing sugar.

SWEETMEATS FOR CANCERIANS
Serves at least Four to Six
1 oz/25g cornflour
16 fl oz/475ml cold water
1 oz/25g caster sugar
1 tablespoon rosewater
1 tablespoon pine kernels, chopped
2 teaspoons unsalted shelled pistachio nuts, chopped

For the syrup
2 oz/50g icing sugar
½ pint/300ml cold water
2 tablespoons rosewater
3 tablespoons raisins
1 tablespoon blanched almonds, halved

Mix the cornflour in a little of the water in a pan. Add the rest of the water and the caster sugar and stir to dissolve. Bring to the boil and cook very gently. Stir all the time and watch that it does not burn. Cook until it thickens into a stiff paste. Stir in the chopped nuts. Pour into an oblong tray that has been rinsed in cold water and left damp. Leave to set. Cut it into 1 inch/2.5 cm squares.

Make an uncooked syrup by dissolving the icing sugar in the cold water. Add the rosewater, raisins and almonds. Put the sweetmeats in a bowl or a dish and pour the syrup over them.

LEO

SUN IN LEO 23 JULY - 22 AUGUST
RULED BY THE SUN

LEO is the ancient royal sign and as such embodies all the traditional regal qualities: pride, courage, initiative, warmth and generosity of spirit. It is also the artistic sign *par excellence* and the true Leo treats every one of life's experiences as a creative challenge. Food is something to be enjoyed and rich cordon bleu cuisine is the ideal fare for the Leo with sufficient money and leisure to support an extravagant life style. Leo is a hot, fiery, dry, masculine sign.

LEO ENVIRONMENTS

Leo rules all steep rocky places, mountains, fortresses and parks, castles and, of course, royal palaces. In fact, anywhere with a sumptuous or regal air is Leonine, including all the grandest hotels and restaurants. Leos like to do things in style, and that includes eating. The dining table is laid with the finest materials, and good taste is sometimes sacrificed in the cause of ostentatious display. They are not embarrassed to make an exhibition of private wealth. Even the breakfast table reflects their desire for show, preferably with food laid out on silver platters. Entertainment is appropriate after dinner and singers, dancers and artistes of all description are welcome at Leo's table.

LEO FOODS

Leo foods are lavish, rich and well presented. The true Leo is more concerned with what food looks like and how it tastes than whether it is healthy. As a hot-dry sign it favours methods of cooking such as baking and barbecuing, but is not really concerned with how food is prepared. Rich sauces and bright colours are important to excite the taste buds. Among the meats, heart is ruled by Leo; and among vegetables and herbs, carrots, nettles, bay, mint, rue and thyme. Other foods associated with this sign are those ruled by the Sun, Leo's planet.

LEMON AND BRAZIL NUT SOUP
Serves Four
8 oz/225g onions
4 oz/125g shelled brazil nuts
2 lemons
2 oz/50g butter
2 pints/1.1 litres chicken stock
salt and pepper
2 fl oz/50ml double cream

Peel and slice the onions; chop the brazil nuts coarsely; take the zest off the lemons, with a sharp knife or potato peeler, avoiding the pith.

Heat the butter in a saucepan and gently fry the onions until they are soft, but not coloured. Add the stock, nuts, lemon zest and seasoning and simmer for 20 minutes.

Put the soup in a blender and process until smooth. Return the soup to the pan, check the seasoning and add the cream before heating.

DEEP FRIED MUSSELS WITH A WALNUT AND SESAME SAUCE
Serves Four
This is a Turkish way of dealing with mussels, and the sauce is one they serve with cold fish. Offer wedges of lemon and some thin batons of raw celery.
40 mussels
4 oz/125g flour plus extra for dusting
1 egg
salt
5 fl oz/150ml beer
For the sauce
4 oz/125g shelled walnuts
juice of 1-2 lemons
4 tablespoons *tahini* — sesame seed paste
2 cloves garlic
salt
2 tablespoons chopped dill

First make the sauce. Coarsely chop the walnuts. Put them, the lemon juice, *tahini*, garlic and salt in a blender or processor and blend until creamy. Add the chopped dill and check the seasoning.

Wash and clean the mussels. Boil them in a large covered pan with 2 tablespoons water until their shells open in about 3 minutes (you may have to cook them in batches). Remove the mussels from their shells. Pat them dry on kitchen paper and dust with flour.

Make a batter by mixing the flour, egg and salt with enough beer to make a thin cream. Dip the mussels in the batter and deep fry in hot oil at 375°F/190°C for about 2 minutes until golden. Serve immediately with the sauce.

CHICKEN LIVER TOAST WITH PINE KERNELS AND A LEAF SALAD
Serves Four
8 oz/225g chicken livers
4 fl oz/120ml milk
2 cloves garlic
2 tablespoons olive oil
salt
squeeze of lemon
2 oz/50g pine kernels
4 tablespoons extra virgin olive oil
8 slices French bread
Salad leaves including *rosso* (red leafed chicory), brown edged cos lettuce, curly endive, lamb's leaves, flat leaved parsley
4 tablespoons French dressing

Remove any bitter gall from the chicken livers. Leave them to soak for 2 to 4 hours in milk.

Drain the chicken livers and pat dry on kitchen paper. Cut them into large dice. Peel 1 garlic clove and chop very finely. Heat the 2 tablespoons oil in a frying pan and fry the garlic with the chicken livers briskly for 1 or 2 minutes until they are just set. Season with salt and lemon juice.

Pound the pine kernels and the other garlic clove in a mortar, or process in a blender, with a pinch of salt. When they are a fine paste, add the virgin olive oil in a thin stream stirring all the while.

Toast the bread. Spread thinly with the pine kernel paste. Spoon the chicken livers on top. Reheat under the grill if necessary.

Toss the salad leaves in the French dressing and serve with the chicken liver toast.

A CURRY AS IN BOMBAY
Serves Four

This curry, inspired by Bombay, is a dry one —
to keep in character with Leo. It has also a
sweet/sour touch from the vinegar in the
marinade. Serve with rice, and some boiled new
potatoes and chopped chives tossed in yoghurt and
don't forget the chutneys.

2 lb/900g boned lamb
1½ inch/4 cm piece fresh ginger root
2 medium onions
4 cloves garlic
1 green chilli
1 teaspoon ground cardamom seeds
1 tablespoon ground coriander
1 teaspoon ground cumin
1 teaspoon ground turmeric
salt
3 fl oz/85ml wine vinegar
4 tablespoons oil

Trim the lamb of all fat, skin and sinews and
cut into cubes; peel and slice the ginger; peel and
chop the onions and garlic; seed and slice the chilli.
In a blender, make a paste of the ginger, onions,
garlic, chilli, spices, salt and vinegar. Marinade the
meat in this paste for 3 to 6 hours. Put everything
into a large pan with the oil and bring to the boil.
Add a little water if it seems excessively dry. Cover
and simmer for at least 45 minutes or until very
tender. Taste and add more salt if necessary.

Uncover the pan and continue cooking, stirring
all the time, until the meat is almost dry. Serve
immediately, but it will keep very well until the
next day.

CALF'S LIVER WITH DUBONNET AND ORANGE
Serves Four

This recipe was written by an English woman, but
the ingredients are quintessentially French. If you
cannot find calf's liver, lamb's will do although its
flavour is usually too strong. Frozen lamb's liver
or liver that is not extremely fresh is not as
satisfactory. Serve with baked tomatoes and a
green salad. For potatoes, you could part boil some
tiny new potatoes and then finish their cooking
in olive oil.

4 shallots
1 tablespoon olive oil
2 oz/50g butter
4 slices of calf's liver, each about 4 oz/125g
salt and black pepper
flour for dusting
1 tablespoon orange juice
grated rind of 1 orange
4 fl oz/120ml Dubonnet
4 fl oz/120ml double cream
squeeze of lemon juice

Peel and finely chop the shallots. Heat the oil
and butter in a frying pan. Add the shallots and
cook them very gently until tender.

Season the liver and dredge with flour. Add to
the pan and cook over gentle heat for not more
than 3 minutes until firm but still pink. Transfer
the liver and shallots to a heated serving dish and
keep warm.

Stir the orange juice, grated rind and Dubonnet
into the pan and boil to reduce by half. Stir in
the cream and boil until thickened. Taste for
seasoning, adding lemon juice if necessary. Pour
the sauce round the liver and serve.

ESCALOPES OF TURKEY WITH LEMON AND PARSLEY
Serves Four

The *gremolata* dressing of lemon, garlic and parsley
is an aromatic touch that is found in Italy. It makes
a grand topping to many a stew and, here, to a
simple grilled dish. You could serve the escalopes
with a fairly assertive vegetable, such as the yellow
peppers, on page 48. Mashed potato, made with
lots of butter and cream, would go well too.

1 tablespoon chopped parsley
1 teaspoon chopped thyme
1 teaspoon chopped marjoram
1 sprig rosemary, chopped
2 shallots, chopped
juice of 1 lemon

5 fl oz/150ml olive oil plus extra for brushing
4 escalopes of turkey breast, each about 4 oz/125g
salt and black pepper
4 fl oz/120ml white wine
4 fl oz/120ml chicken stock
For the gremolata *dressing*
grated rind of 1 lemon
bunch of parsley, chopped
1 clove garlic, peeled and chopped

Make a marinade by mixing the chopped herbs with the shallots, lemon juice and olive oil. Put the escalopes in a dish with the marinade. Leave for 1 hour, turning once.

Remove the escalopes from the marinade and season with salt and pepper. Grill under a high heat for about 3 minutes per side (depending on the thickness of the turkey). Brush with olive oil when necessary.

Meanwhile, put the marinade in a small pan and cook uncovered for 3 minutes over high heat. Add the white wine and chicken stock and boil to reduce by half. Taste for salt and pepper.

For the *gremolata* dressing mix the ingredients together.

Transfer the escalopes to a serving dish. Strain the marinade over them. Scatter the *gremolata* over the top and serve.

BEEF WITH MUSTARD SAUCE
Serves Four

It seems sometimes that steak and chips is the French national dish and this is a roasted and more decorous version with a yellow sauce to keep it Leonine. I have allowed 6 ounces/175g of meat per person but this is in the context of a three or four course meal. If serving nothing else, more may be thought necessary. Serve with fried potatoes or crisps and perhaps some yellow courgettes.

1½ lb/700g sirloin or fillet of beef in one piece
salt and black pepper
oil

For the sauce
1 tablespoon brandy
4 fl oz/120ml white wine

3 fl oz/85ml water
2 tablespoons Dijon mustard
5 fl oz/150ml double cream
salt and pepper
2 oz/50g butter, cut in small pieces

Trim the sirloin or fillet of sinew, excess fat or skin. Season and rub with oil. Heat a heavy pan to smoking and sear the beef over high heat. Put the pan in a preheated oven at 450°F/230°C/Gas Mark 8 for 20 minutes for rare. Remove the beef and leave it to rest on a covered dish.

Pour off any surplus fat from the pan. Put the pan over medium heat. Warm the brandy, set it alight and pour it into the pan. When the flame subsides add the wine and water. Boil to reduce by two-thirds over high heat. Stir in the mustard and cream. Boil further, until the sauce is thick and smooth. Taste for seasoning. Then over a low heat, whisk in the butter piece by piece. Carve the beef and serve with the sauce.

AUBERGINES SWEET AND SOUR — CAPONATA
Serves Four

That mixture of the acid and the sweet so beloved of Leo is here shown off by a dish that comes from southern Italy, particularly Sicily. It makes a great contribution to a vegetarian meal and can be offered with plainly roasted meat.

1 large aubergine
1 onion
1 clove garlic
1 green pepper
1 stick celery
6 tablespoons olive oil
2 teaspoons wine vinegar
2 teaspoons sugar
2 teaspoons tomato purée
salt and black pepper
10 stoned black olives
3 teaspoons capers
4 fillets anchovy, cut in pieces

Top and tail the aubergine. Cut into ¼ inch/5mm slices. Sprinkle with salt and leave in a colander under a weighted plate for 30 minutes. Rinse and dry with kitchen paper.

Peel or prepare and chop the onion, garlic, pepper and celery. Heat 2 tablespoons of the oil in a saucepan. Add the chopped vegetables and fry gently until tender. Add the vinegar, sugar, tomatoe purée and seasoning. Cover the pan and cook for 10 minutes over low heat.

Cut the olives in half. Add them and the capers to the pan. Take the pan off the heat.

Grease a baking tray with some oil and put the aubergine slices on it in one layer. Spoon the cooked mixture onto each slice. Pour a little oil round the slices. Cook in a preheated oven at 300°F/150°C/Gas Mark 2 for 20 to 30 minutes until the aubergine is tender. Decorate with small pieces of anchovy. Serve hot, warm or cool; immediately or the next day.

YELLOW PEPPERS BAKED WITH ANCHOVIES
Serves Four
A yellow vegetable for the sun. Eat it with mashed potato, and with something fairly light.

Beef with Mustard Sauce

4 yellow peppers
1 oz/25g butter
3 fl oz/85ml olive oil
salt and pepper
1 tablespoon chopped marjoram
3 cloves garlic, chopped
8 fillets anchovy, chopped

Grill the peppers to make the skin blister. Rub off the skin. Halve the peppers and remove the stalks, seeds and pith. Cut into longitudinal slices.

Melt the butter in the oil in an ovenproof dish. Put in the pepper slices, season with salt and pepper and scatter the marjoram, garlic and anchovies over the top. Cover with aluminium foil and bake in a preheated oven at 350°F/180°C/Gas Mark 4 for up to 15 minutes (the time will depend on how much they were cooked by the skinning process). Serve hot, warm or cool.

A SWEET SOUR SALAD OF CARROTS
Serves Four
1 lb/450g young carrots
4 tablespoons olive oil
juice of 1 lemon
1 tablespoon rosewater
1 tablespoon honey
pinch salt
1 teaspoon ground cinnamon
4 oz/125g raisins

Scrub and grate the carrots. In a salad bowl, make a dressing with the oil, lemon juice and rosewater. Mix in the honey, salt and cinnamon. Add the raisins and carrots and toss to mix.

PICKLED LEMONS IN THE ARAB FASHION
Fills one 2 lb/900g jar approx.
A wonderfully simple pickle — starting yellow, finishing pink-red, that goes with many things.
4 medium lemons
3 oz/75g salt.
2 teaspoons paprika
vegetable oil

Scrub the lemons to rid them of coating and chemicals. Cut them into thin slices, removing the pips. Lay them in a single layer on a flat board or dish angled to allow the water to drain away. Sprinkle with salt. Leave them for 24 to 36 hours in the cool.

Sterilize the jar. Pack the drained and dried lemon in layers with a little paprika over each layer. Cover the top with oil. Seal the jar and leave for at least 3 weeks.

HEARTS OF CREAM WITH CANDIED ORANGE
Serves Four
A very simple way of cooking from France, the centrepiece of which requires no cooking at all. You do, however, need 4 little heart-shaped porcelain or aluminium moulds, with holes pierced in the bottom. You will also need some clean pieces of muslin to line them with. You can make your own moulds by piercing holes in plastic cartons, but they won't be heart-shaped. Eat them with the orange sauce given here or a plain thick cream and caster sugar can be offered as well.
10 fl oz/300ml double cream
2 egg whites
For the orange sauce
2 oranges, for their zest
6 oz/175g sugar
10 fl oz/300ml water
approximately 2 fl oz/50ml Orange Curaçao
juice of 1 orange

Line the moulds with muslin. Whip the cream until firm. Whip the egg whites to soft peaks and fold into the cream. Spoon the mixture into the moulds. Fold the muslin over the tops. Leave to drain on a tray in the cool until the following day.

To make the sauce, remove the zests from the oranges in ribbons with a swivel peeler. Make sure there is absolutely no pith. Put the zests in a saucepan with ample cold water and bring to the boil. Drain and repeat twice more. When cool, cut into very thin strips.

In a saucepan over medium heat, dissolve the sugar in the water. Bring to a rolling boil and cook, uncovered, for 4 minutes. Add the zests and boil, uncovered, for 10 to 15 minutes until the syrup has thickened. The syrup should be thick but not setting. When the syrup is cool add the Curaçao and orange juice.

Unfold the muslin and turn the cream hearts out onto cold plates. Serve cold (it is better if they are not refrigerated) with the sauce.

PEACHES WITH LEMON AND BRANDY
Serves Six
A delicious summer dish, when peaches are at their best.
1 lb/450g granulated sugar
1 pint/600ml water
1 large lemon
6 ripe peaches
4 tablespoons brandy

Combine the sugar and the water in a saucepan. Stir to dissolve the sugar over low heat. Then boil for 4 minutes.

Top and tail the lemon and cut into 12 slices. Add the lemon slices to the syrup and boil uncovered for 10 minutes.

Skin the peaches by dipping for 20 seconds into boiling water. Poach them over a low heat in the now simmering syrup until they are tender. This may take 10 minutes or more, depending on their ripeness and size. When the peaches are cooked, remove to a bowl with a slotted spoon and set aside in a cool place.

Continue to cook the syrup and lemon slices, uncovered, until the lemon is transparent and the syrup reduced by half. Set aside to cool.

Spoon the brandy over each peach. Pour the syrup and lemon slices into the bowl. Serve (and eat) the lemon as well as the peaches.

APRICOT TOAST
Serves Four
4 slices white bread
3 oz/75g unsalted butter
8 apricots
4 oz/125g vanilla sugar
apricot brandy or kirsch

Butter the bread. Grease well an ovenproof dish.

Halve the apricots and remove their stones. Press 4 halves into each slice of bread, skin side downwards. Put sugar where the stones were. Put a drop of liqueur on each half fruit. Bake in a preheated oven at 350°F/180°C/Gas Mark 4 for about 30 minutes until golden.

Serve immediately.

GRATIN OF SATSUMAS
Serves Four
Another citrus fruit for Leo, in a classic French *sabayon* sauce, presented in a modern manner.
5 satsumas
12 muscatel grapes
4 egg yolks
1 tablespoon Grand Marnier
1 tablespoon caster sugar
icing sugar for glazing

Squeeze the juice from one satsuma and reserve 2 tablespoons for the sauce. Peel and section the others, tidy up any excess pith and cut away the pithy cores. Peel, halve and pip the grapes.

Set a bowl over a saucepan of simmering water. Put in the egg yolks, satsuma juice, Grand Marnier and caster sugar and beat for 10 minutes until the mixture foams and coats the whisk.

On 4 heated ovenproof plates arrange the satsumas in a circle with the grapes in the centre. Spoon the sauce over the satsumas and sprinkle all over with icing sugar. Glaze evenly under a hot grill for about 2 minutes. Serve immediately.

VIRGO

SUN IN VIRGO 23 AUGUST - 23 SEPTEMBER
RULED BY MERCURY

VIRGO is the sign of the virgin, the archetypal symbol of purity. In practice Virgoans are hard workers and take on more than their share of domestic and professional responsibilities. They are more involved in the day to day preparation of food than any other sign with the possible exception of Cancer. People born with the Moon in Virgo are often in charge of the kitchen. This is a cold, dry sign and rules the harvest.

VIRGO ENVIRONMENTS

Virgo is the sign of work, so in the countryside it rules cultivated fields, especially corn fields. In the home it is associated with those places where food is actually prepared. When they sit down to eat Virgos are more concerned with cleanliness than comfort and take more notice of what is in their food than what it looks like. Places of work are Virgoan and so are works or office canteens. For a special meal out true Virgos appreciate a visit to a restaurant in the country, where the service is good and the decor plain but tasteful. Loud music and noisy company upsets the Virgoan digestion.

VIRGO FOODS

Together with Cancer, Virgo rules the digestive process, and Virgoans are often fussy, either by choice or necessity, over their diets. The modern health food industry which seeks a return to food uncontaminated by artificial chemicals is profoundly Virgoan. Wholefoods and all healthy meals (preferably homemade) come under this sign. Food is often plain rather than rich; and, for health reasons, small portions are preferred. Their concern with pure food sometimes leads to the use of overrefined products, but today wholefoods are more likely to predominate in their diet. The Virgoan virgin is often shown holding a sheaf of corn — the Sun is in Virgo at harvest time — and the sign is associated with grains, and hence bread, biscuits and pastry, as well as with game birds and all berries, seeds and herbs in general. Foods ruled by Mercury are also associated with Virgo.

EGGS WRAPPED WITH LAMB
Serves Four

Just as cabbage rolls travelled from Turkey to Sweden, so the idea of eggs wrapped in meat seems to have travelled from India to Scotland, whence they have spread to every public house in Britain. This dish is usually served with a spicy tomato sauce; some Arab bread would also be good as an accompaniment.

12 oz/350g lean trimmed lamb
1 onion
2 oz/50g soft breadcrumbs
2 tablespoons chopped parsley
1 teaspoon ground cinnamon
salt and black pepper
4 hard-boiled eggs
eggwash made with 1 egg
1 cup dried breadcrumbs or matzo meal
oil for deep frying

Grind the meat in the food processor to a paste. Or, mince it twice through the finest plate of a mincing machine. Peel and chop the onion extremely fine. Mix the meat, onion, soft breadcrumbs, parsley, cinnamon, salt and pepper to a mouldable consistency. Divide into 4 and flatten each to a disc. Peel the hard boiled eggs. Dip them in the eggwash and place each on a disc. Wrap the meat paste round the egg, moulding and pressing to cover it completely. Roll the meat covered eggs in the matzo meal. Deep fry at 375°F/190°C for about 5 minutes, turning at least once. Drain on kitchen paper, place on a serving dish and serve halved.

A MEZE
Serves Four

This first course is quite elaborate in the making, needing a strong arm to pound and press or a food processor in good condition. It should be served with fresh bread or Arab bread to mop up the flavours and the purées, a plate of tomato salad, dressed with a mint and parsley vinaigrette and sprinkled with finely chopped cucumber, and a bowl of olives. Of course, each element (proportionately enlarged) could be served as a first course in its own right, or the collection could be expanded to make a whole meal, with the addition perhaps of something crunchy in texture to add variety to the purées and custards. Virgoans like small portions, this combination, like the northern *smörg°asbord* or the French hors d'oeuvre, is likely to suit them very well.

Aubergine caviar
1 small aubergine, about 12 oz/350g
salt
2 fl oz/50ml olive oil
1 clove garlic
1 small bunch parsley, flat leaved is best
lemon juice
pepper

Slice the aubergine, sprinkle with salt and leave to drain in a colander under a weighted plate for 30 minutes. Rinse and pat dry. Heat the olive oil in a frying pan and fry the aubergine until tender and lightly coloured. Put the aubergine and the oil through a sieve or the fine plate of a food mill.

Crush the garlic; wash, dry, and chop the parsley.

Mix the aubergine with the garlic and parsley and season with the lemon juice, salt (if necessary), and black pepper.

An aubergine, coconut and cumin custard
12 oz/350g aubergine
2 cloves garlic
1 tablespoon olive oil
2 eggs
8 fl oz/250ml yoghurt or sour cream
pinch ground cumin
salt and pepper
1 oz/25g grated creamed coconut

Peel and slice the aubergine; peel and chop the garlic finely. Steam the aubergine for 15 to 25 minutes or until tender. Heat the olive oil and cook the garlic very gently for 2 to 3 minutes. Chop the steamed aubergine and put it in a bowl. Mix in the garlic, oil and the rest of the ingredients. Taste for seasoning. Spoon the mixture into a small non-stick loaf tin and cover with aluminium foil.

Stand the loaf tin in a baking dish. Pour in enough hot water to come two-thirds up the sides of the loaf tin. Put the baking dish in an oven set at 250°F/120°C/Gas Mark ½ and bake for 1 hour. If after 1 hour the mixture is still a little liquid continue cooking for a further 10 minutes.

Cool the custard. Turn it out of the mould and serve in slices.

Tapenade
24 black olives, pitted
2 oz/50g tuna
8 anchovy fillets
1 tablespoon capers
1 teaspoon Dijon mustard
a squeeze of lemon juice
2 fl oz/50ml olive oil
1 teaspoon brandy
black pepper
chopped parsley or coriander

Pound the olives in a mortar. Add the fishes and the capers. Pound again. It should be a rough textured purée. Add the mustard and lemon juice and whisk in the oil. Add the brandy and pepper and taste. Sprinkle with chopped parsley or coriander.

Taramasalata
4 oz/125g smoked cod's roe
4 oz/125g full fat cream cheese
½ clove garlic
lemon juice
black pepper
2 fl oz/50ml olive oil
single cream

Put the cod's roe and the cream cheese through a fine sieve into a bowl. Peel and crush the garlic and add it along with some lemon juice and black pepper.

With a wooden spoon, stir in the olive oil, adding it in a thin stream as if for a mayonnaise.

Check the consistency, if it is too stiff add a little single cream. Taste and adjust seasoning.

Brandade of smoked mackerel
1 small clove garlic
6 oz/175g smoked mackerel fillet
2 fl oz/50ml olive oil
2 fl oz/50ml milk
salt and pepper
lemon juice
chopped black olives

This is best done in the mortar, the food processor makes too fine a purèe.

Peel and pound the garlic with a pinch of salt. Skin the mackerel and check for bones. Add to the mortar and pound until smooth. Transfer this paste to a bowl. Put the bowl over a saucepan of hot water.

Warm the oil and milk in separate pans. Stirring with a wooden spoon, add them little by little, in alternate streams, to the mackerel. You should aim for a light emulsion, fluffy rather than sloppy. Season to taste. Decorate with some chopped black olives. Serve warm.

CHICKEN IN SHRIMP AND ALMOND SAUCE FROM BRAZIL
Serves Four toi Six
You may need to shop at a West Indian speciality store for the dried shrimp and the palm oil. These are essential for any evocation of the tastes of the province of Bahia in Brazil.
8 oz/225g desiccated coconut, for coconut milk
15 fl oz/450ml water
1 onion
1 clove garlic
2 tomatoes
1 hot chilli
2 fl oz/50ml vegetable oil
salt and pepper
juice of ½ lemon
2 tablespoons chopped fresh coriander
1 large chicken, jointed
¾ pint/450ml stock
4 oz/125g ground almonds
4 oz/125g dried shrimp, ground fine

2 oz/50g creamed coconut
2 tablespoons palm oil

Put the desiccated coconut into a pan with the water. Heat just to boiling point. Remove from the heat and pour into a blender. Blend vigorously for 30 seconds, then press through a sieve. Throw away the residue and reserve the liquid.

Prepare the vegetables: peel and chop the onion and garlic; skin and seed the tomatoes; seed and chop the chilli. Heat the olive oil in a large casserole, add the vegetables and cook until tender. Season with salt and pepper. Add the lemon juice and chopped coriander.

Add the chicken to the casserole. Add the stock and bring to the boil. Lower the heat, cover tightly and cook gently for 25 minutes or until tender. Remove the chicken pieces and leave to cool.

When the chicken pieces are cool, remove carefully all vestiges of skin and bone and cut the chicken into rough cubes.

Drain the contents of the casserole well and reserve the liquid. Discard the vegetables.

In another pan, place the ground almonds and the dried shrimp. Add to them the coconut milk and the reserved liquid. Simmer for 15 minutes, then add the creamed coconut to impart a gloss to the chicken. Add the chicken pieces and the palm oil, check for seasoning and heat through without boiling.

A Meze

GRILLED BREAST OF GUINEA FOWL WITH ORANGE AND LIME
Serves Four

This dish has become one of the standard bearers of French *nouvelle cuisine*. Offer it with some mange tout peas plainly cooked, served on a bed of Webb's lettuce heart.

3 oz/75g onion
3 tablespoons orange juice
3 tablespoons lime juice
7 tablespoons chicken stock
4 breasts guinea fowl, with skin
1 tablespoon granulated sugar
4 tablespoons wine vinegar
1 tablespoon double cream
salt and black pepper
zest of 1 lime
olive oil

Peel and chop the onion finely. Mix the onion, orange and lime juice with the stock. Put the breasts to marinate in this mixture for 3 to 6 hours, turning every hour.

Remove the breasts, taking care not to remove the skin, and set aside while you make the sauce with the marinade.

Cook the marinade in a tightly covered pan over gentle heat for 15 minutes.

In a small pan, heat the sugar until it caramelizes. Pour in the vinegar stirring to mix (tilt the pan away from you to avoid splashes and burns). Stir in the marinade, cream and seasoning. Keep the mixture warm.

Take the zest off the lime avoiding the pith. Add it to a pan of cold water, bring to the boil, uncovered, and cook for 3 minutes. Drain and repeat. Drain and cut into very thin strips.

Season the guinea fowl breasts with salt and pepper and brush with oil. Grill them under a high heat beginning with the underside. Brush with oil as you turn the breasts. Grill for approximately 7 minutes on each side. The breasts should brown well, but not burn.

Serve the breasts with a very little of the sauce and decorated with the lime zest strips.

CARROTS WITH DRIED FRUIT
Serves Four

In Russia, they think of the carrot as primarily a sweet vegetable, as indeed it should be, and emphasize its character with sweet-sour combinations. This would go well with a plain bean dish in a vegetarian meal.

4 oz/125g mixed raisins, dried apricots and prunes
1 lb/450g carrots
1 oz/25g butter
½ pint/300ml water
2 tablespoons sour cream
salt and black pepper

Soak the fruit and remove stones; peel and slice the carrots lengthwise.

Melt the butter in a saucepan. Add the carrots and cook gently for 2 minutes. Add the water and the fruit. Simmer, covered, until tender.

With a slotted spoon transfer the carrots and fruit to a serving dish. Reduce the liquid in the pan to a few spoonfuls by boiling hard. Lower the temperature and stir in the sour cream. Season and pour over carrots and fruit.

SPINACH AND SORREL PANCAKES
Serves Four

Sorrel is a Virgoan herb. It is here combined with spinach and cream cheese to make a vegetable side dish. It can also be offered as a first course or extended to make a vegetarian main dish. It is deceptively simple.

For the pancakes
4 oz/125g flour
2 eggs, beaten
8 fl oz/250ml milk
2 oz/50g butter plus extra for the pan
salt and pepper
For the filling
8 oz/225g spinach
1 oz/25g sorrel
1 oz/25g butter plus extra for the dish and brushing
4 oz/125g cream cheese
salt and black pepper
single cream, if needed

Mix the flour, beaten eggs and half the milk together in a bowl. Melt the butter and mix it into the batter. Add as much of the rest of the milk as is needed to make a batter the consistency of thin cream.

Grease a 6 inch/15 cm frying pan with a little butter and put over a medium to high heat. When hot pour in sufficient batter to cover the bottom thinly, twisting the hot pan as you pour to get a rapid spread. After about 30 seconds the bottom of the pancake will be golden brown. Turn it over and cook the other side on a lower heat until browning in spots. Grease the pan again when necessary, usually after every third pancake. Pile the pancakes up as you cook them. They will keep, wrapped in aluminium foil in the refrigerator, for 2 or 3 days. This batter will make at least 8 pancakes.

To make the filling, wash and dry the spinach and sorrel. Heat the butter in a pan and cook the spinach and sorrel, covered, for 5 minutes until tender. Purée in a processor or through a food mill or sieve. Mix with the cream cheese and season well. If too thick add a little single cream.

Lay the pancakes flat on the work surface and place a tablespoon of filling across each of them. Roll up like cigars. Butter an oven dish and lay the pancakes in it. Brush their tops with melted butter. Cover with foil or a lid and place in a preheated oven at 350°F/180°C/Gas Mark 4 for about 10 minutes until thoroughly hot.

GNOCCHI WITH A PARSLEY BUTTER SAUCE
Serves Four

Mercury is especially identified with grains. This is the justification for suggesting this Italian dish of gnocchi though here the farinaceous base has almost been lost beneath the cream cheese.

8 oz/22g cream cheese
2 eggs, beaten
4 oz/125g grated Parmesan cheese, plus extra for serving
3 oz/75g flour
2 oz/50g butter, melted

salt and pepper
nutmeg
For the sauce
4 oz/125g butter
juice of ½ lemon
2 tablespoons chopped parsley
salt and pepper

Sieve the cream cheese into a bowl. Mix in the rest of the ingredients and beat well. Or process all the ingredients in a food processor.

On a well floured surface, fashion the mixture into rolls the thickness of a Frankfurter sausage. Cut into 1 inch/2.5 cm lengths. Keep the gnocchi well floured to avoid sticking.

Bring a large pan of salted water to the simmer. Drop in the gnocchi and cook for about 5 minutes or until they rise to the surface. Do not overcrowd the pan. Take the gnocchi out as they cook with a slotted spoon. Drain on kitchen paper, cover and keep warm.

To make the sauce melt the butter in a pan with 3 tablespoons water and the lemon juice. Boil for 1 minute. Add the parsley and seasoning. Pour over the gnocchi. Serve with Parmesan for sprinkling to taste.

WALNUT CAKE WITH FIGS AND CREAM
Serves Four

butter and flour for the cake tin
3 oz/75g shelled walnuts
2 oz/50g soft white breadcrumbs
6 eggs
4 oz/125g caster sugar
For the filling
4 oz/125g unsalted butter
4 oz/125g caster sugar
2 fl oz/50ml sour cream

To serve
12 figs in syrup
10 fl oz/300ml sour cream or whipped double cream

Line an 8 inch/20 cm cake tin with buttered greaseproof paper, or butter and flour a tin with a removable bottom.

Chop the walnuts medium fine and mix with the breadcrumbs. Separate the eggs into 2 bowls. Beat the yolks with the sugar until a pale yellow and thick enough to leave a ribbon trail when the whisk is lifted. Mix in the walnuts and breadcrumbs. Beat the whites to a stiff peak and fold in. Turn the mixture into the cake tin and bake for approximately 1 hour in a preheated oven at 350°F/180°C/Gas Mark 4. Test with a skewer. Take the cake out of the tin and cool on a rack.

To make the filling, cream the butter and sugar. Beat in the sour cream and leave in the refrigerator to firm up. Split the cake in two and fill with the butter cream.

Serve the cake with a dish of figs preserved in syrup and a bowl of thick soured cream or stiffly whipped double cream.

RICOTTA AL CAFFE
Serves Four
¾ oz/20g high roasted coffee beans
6 oz/175g cream cheese
2 oz/50g caster sugar
1 fl oz/25 ml dark rum
single cream, if needed
For serving
double cream
langues de chat

Grind the coffee beans to a fineness suitable for Turkish coffee. Beat together with the cream cheese, sugar and rum. If the mixture is too stiff thin it with a little single cream. Taste and add more sugar if necessary.

Serve in tiny bowls, one for each person, with a dish of lightly whipped double cream and some thin sweet biscuits such as langues de chat.

BARLEY CREAM
Serves Four
Barley cream is best when served with a compote of fruit, perhaps apples or greengages, and some sponge fingers.

2 oz/50g pearl barley
1 pint/600ml single cream
1 tablespoon cornflour
1 tablespoon milk
2 large eggs
2 teaspoons orange flower water
2 oz/50g caster sugar or to taste

Boil the pearl barley in water for about 20 minutes until it is tender. Put the cream in a pan. Drain the barley and add to the cream and simmer gently.

Mix the cornflour with the milk. Beat the eggs and mix in the cornflour and the orange flower water. Take the barley cream off the heat and slowly add the egg mixture, stirring all the while. Return to the heat and cook, stirring, until the mixture thickens. Do not let it boil, but hold at a simmer. Add sugar to taste. Pour into custard glasses or small bowls and refrigerate.

YOGHURT
Serves Four to Eight
Your own yoghurt, once you have the rhythm of making it, is usually sweeter and cleaner. Remember to have all the utensils sterile, washed in boiling water. Serve yoghurt on its own, with sugar, with black cherry jam or with honey.
1¾ pints/1 litre milk
2 tablespoons plain live yoghurt, as a starter

Bring the milk to the boil in a saucepan. Simmer it slowly for about 15 minutes until it has lost one-third of its volume. Cool the milk to 106-109°F/41-43°C. Use a thermometer.

Put the yoghurt starter (if you use more it will be too sour) in a clean bowl. Add 2 tablespoons of the milk and stir to dissolve. Add the rest of the milk, stirring. Cover the bowl with clingfilm. Wrap it in towels or blankets or put it in an insulated box. Leave it in a warm place, from 80 to 90°F/27 to 33°C, such as an airing cupboard for 6 to 8 hours, until the fermentation is sufficient. If you leave it too long the yoghurt will be too sour. Keep it in the refrigerator. To make a new batch, use some of the old yoghurt, not more than four days old, as the starter.

LIBRA

SUN IN LIBRA 23 SEPTEMBER - 23 OCTOBER
RULED BY VENUS

LIBRA is a delicate and peaceful sign, ruled by Venus the classical goddess of love. The Libran's greatest skill lies in bringing people together and creating an atmosphere in which a pleasant experience is more or less guaranteed. Librans excel in arranging small gatherings, such as intimate breakfast or dinner parties, and their attention to detail is unparalleled. They aim for perfection, so are often disappointed. They are quite sensitive, and likely to be happier in small groups. Their friends, on whom they rely a great deal, tend to be civilized, sensitive and discreet. Libra is a hot, moist, air sign.

LIBRA ENVIRONMENTS
The Libran restaurant or dining room is peaceful, quiet, tastefully lit and beautifully furnished. In fact, the atmosphere is often more important than the food in ensuring a pleasant evening. Librans like to frequent fashionable eating places, or those close to cultural centres. Delicatessens and confectioneries are also ideal Libran haunts. Libra also rules cultivated highlands and orchards.

LIBRA FOODS
Librans are famous for their love of sweet things and all cakes and confectioneries come under this sign. Ideally, Libran food should be light, pleasantly presented and easy to digest. Libra rules birds in general; sweet pigeon pie, which is a delicacy in Morocco, is typical of this sign. It also rules kidneys. Foods ruled by Venus are also associated with Libra.

JAPANESE ASPARAGUS SALAD
Serves Four

This is a very light first course, although you could double the quantities if you have a taste for the crunchy spears, which resemble peas in taste because they are only just cooked.

For the best flavour and texture the asparagus should be freshly cut.

24 thin spears of green asparagus
salt
2 teaspoons mustard powder
1 tablespoon water
1 egg yolk
1 teaspoon light soy sauce

Prepare the asparagus. Cut off their hard stems, trim and peel the bottoms if necessary. Cook in a wide pan of boiling salt water for 3 to 4 minutes or until just tender, but still crunchy. Drain and refresh under cold water. Cut the asparagus across in two.

In a salad bowl, mix the mustard and water. Add the egg yolk and soy sauce and stir well. Toss the spears in this dressing, arrange on plates and serve.

SOUR PRAWN SOUP
Serves Four

Libra is a hot-moist sign, so soups are its most suitable food. This soup is inspired by a recipe from Thailand. Thai fish sauce is available in some delicatessens and Southeast Asian food shops. If it is not available use soy sauce instead.

1 lb/450g fresh or frozen unshelled prawns
2 tablespoons sesame oil
2 pints/1.1 litres water
zest and juice of 1 lemon
salt
3 fresh chillis, seeded
1 tablespoon Thai fish sauce
4 tomatoes
4 spring onions
1 tablespoon chopped fresh coriander

Shell and devein the prawns.

Heat the sesame oil in a pan and fry the prawn heads and shells. Add the water, lemon zest, salt and 2 of the chillis. Bring to the boil and cook uncovered for 30 minutes. Strain and return liquid to the heat.

Add the fish sauce, lemon juice and the prawns if fresh. Simmer very lightly for 10 minutes. If the prawns are frozen only add them at the last minute.

Skin, seed and chop the tomatoes finely; chop the remaining chilli very fine. Chop the spring onions in rounds. Stir all these and the coriander into the soup and serve immediately.

CHICKEN AND CUCUMBER SALAD
Serves Four

Libra is a moist sign under Venus. Many of the recipes, therefore, are balanced, succulent and light. In this simple yet tasty salad I have used the breast of the chicken (in homage to the mothering aspects of Venus) and the cucumber is in tune with the succulence favoured for vegetables and fruit.

8 dried Chinese mushrooms
2 small breasts of chicken, off the bone
1 pint/600ml cold chicken stock
1 cucumber
1 tablespoon light soy sauce
1 tablespoon sesame oil
1 tablespoon dry sherry
3 teaspoons mustard powder
salt
sugar

Soak the mushrooms in hot water for about 20 minutes. Squeeze out the water. Remove and discard the stalks. Put the chicken breasts and the mushrooms in the cold stock in a covered pan. Bring to the boil and simmer gently for approximately 10 minutes until cooked. Remove the chicken breasts and cut into strips. Remove the mushrooms and reserve with the chicken. Split the cucumber lengthwise, remove the seeds and cut into thin slices. Reserve.

Make the dressing by mixing together the soy, oil, sherry, mustard and seasoning. Let stand for 10 minutes. Pour over the chicken strips and mushrooms and toss. Let this stand for another

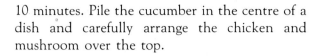

10 minutes. Pile the cucumber in the centre of a dish and carefully arrange the chicken and mushroom over the top.

SQUAB STIR-FRIED WITH MANGE TOUT PEAS
Serves Four

A very light Chinese dish, using the luxury flesh of the squab — young pigeons raised in captivity. Wood pigeons will not do. You can substitute chicken. Eat this with plain rice, or have it as part of a composite main course, in the Chinese manner. It is best to use a wok as deep frying is not easy in a normal frying pan.

2 squab, about 15 oz/425g each
3 tablespoons medium sherry
2 teaspoons cornflour
1 egg white, lightly beaten
salt
1½ teaspoons sugar
2 tablespoons light soy sauce
4 spring onions
2 cloves garlic
8 oz/225g mange tout peas
10 fl oz/300ml vegetable oil for frying
4 thin slices peeled fresh ginger root
3 tablespoons chicken stock or water

Skin the squab and cut the flesh into dice. Place it in a bowl with 1 tablespoon of the sherry, 1 teaspoon of the cornflour, the egg white, salt and ½ teaspoon of the sugar. Stir to coat the flesh. Cover and leave for 30 minutes.

In a small bowl combine the soy sauce, the remaining sherry, salt and the rest of the sugar. Stir to dissolve. Leave in reserve for the sauce later in the cooking.

Cut the spring onions into rounds; peel and chop the garlic; string the mange tout peas and blanch for 20 seconds in boiling water. Drain and refresh under cold water. Pat dry with kitchen paper. Reserve.

Heat the oil in a wok to hot but not smoking. Add the squab and fry, trying to keep the pieces separate, for 30 seconds. Lift out with a slotted spoon and reserve. Put the ginger and the mange tout peas to cook in the same oil for 20 seconds. Lift out and reserve.

Drain the oil leaving only 1 tablespoonful in the wok. Return the wok to the heat. Add the spring onions and garlic. Fry for a few seconds. Add the pigeon and continue to fry for 20 seconds over high heat. Add the reserved sauce, cook until it bubbles, then add the chicken stock.

Meanwhile mix the remaining teaspoon of cornflour in a spoonful of water and stir into the pan. Add the mange tout peas and ginger and cook briefly, tossing to get everything well coated.

CHICKEN SAVOYARDE
Serves Four

This Libran chicken dish is from the Savoy region of France. It is quite rich, the sort of thing for a winter's night, and needs mashed potatoes and plain refreshing vegetables as foils to the butter and cheese. Remember to make the stock in advance.

1 chicken, about 3 lb/1.4 kg, divided in 4 joints
salt and black pepper
4 oz/125g butter
10 fl oz/300ml chicken stock, made from the
    chicken carcase and giblets
10 fl oz/300ml dry white wine
bouquet garni of thyme and parsley
1 oz/25g flour
6 fl oz/175ml double cream
4 oz/125g Gruyère cheese, grated
nutmeg
2 oz/50g soft breadcrumbs

Season the chicken joints and brown them in 3 ounces/75g of the butter in a heavy casserole. Add the stock, white wine and herbs. Bring to the boil and simmer very gently for about 30 minutes, until tender. Remove the chicken pieces to a flameproof dish and keep warm.

Strain the cooking liquour and skim off any fat. Melt the remaining butter in the casserole and add the flour. Stir to mix. Gradually stir in 10 fluid ounces/300 ml of the cooking liquor. Cook for 5 minutes, stirring. Stir in the double cream. Add

3 ounces/75g of the cheese and a pinch of nutmeg, adjust seasoning and cook very gently for 5 minutes.

Pour the sauce over the chicken joints. Mix the remaining cheese with the breadcrumbs and scatter over the whole dish then brown under a medium to hot grill.

SOLE SIMMERED IN SAKE
Serves Two

This delicate Japanese way of cooking fish is difficult to cook for more than two people at a time unless you have a kitchen equipped with enough large flat pans to hold several whole flatfish. As well as sole, you can treat flounders, dabs, turbot or brill (cut into portions) the same way. Serve with rice.

2 soles, each about 10 oz/275g
4 fl oz/120ml *mirin* — Japanese sweet rice wine
4 fl oz/120ml *sake* — Japanese rice wine
6 fl oz/175ml chicken stock
4 tablespoons soy sauce
sugar
1 tablespoon chopped chives *or* 1 seeded and sliced
   green chilli

Leave the heads and fins on the fish. Score the black sides with 3 diagonal cuts. Combine the *mirin* and the *sake* in a large pan. Warm the wine and set alight. When the flames subside, add the chicken stock and soy sauce. Season with sugar to taste. Lay the fish in the pan. Cover the fish with a piece of aluminium foil pressing it down. Then cover the pan itself with more foil and a lid. (This double covering is necessary to concentrate the steam onto the fish, to impregnate the flesh with flavour.) Cook for 8 to 10 minutes over a medium high heat. Lift the fish onto plates and pour round the sauce. Decorate with either the chives or green chilli.

SWEETCORN PANCAKES
Serves Four

Sweetcorn pancakes are common as a side dish throughout Southeast Asia, their spicing varying from country to country. Those I describe here are inspired by Indonesia. They make an excellent spicy accompaniment. The recipe suggests using canned sweetcorn, for the sake of availability. Fresh cobs would be nearer the original, but try to make sure they really are fresh.

14 oz/400g can sweetcorn or 4-6 whole corn cobs
2 fresh chillis
1 medium sweet onion
2 cloves garlic
1 teaspoon ground coriander
1 egg
salt
2 fl oz/50ml vegetable oil

Drain the sweetcorn or if you are using fresh corn, boil them and strip off the kernels. Reserve 2 tablespoons of the kernels. Peel and chop the onion; seed the chillis; peel the garlic. Put all the ingredients except the reserved corn and the oil in a blender and purée. Turn out into a bowl and mix in the reserved corn.

Heat the oil in a frying pan. Drop the mixture, tablespoon by tablespoon, into the pan, flattening out to make little fritters. Fry over medium heat for 2 to 3 minutes on each side. Drain on kitchen paper and serve hot.

GRATIN OF POTATOES SAVOYARD
Serves Six

In that corner of France known as Savoy there are delicious potato dishes where the thinly sliced potatoes are baked in the oven with cheese or cream. The *gratin dauphinois* is made with cream and garlic, the *gratin savoyard* has cheese and stock and no garlic. Gruyère is the best cheese to use outside the Savoy.

2 lb/900g potatoes
salt and black pepper
grated nutmeg
3 oz/75g butter
8 oz/225g Gruyère, grated
8 fl oz/250ml chicken or beef stock

Peel the potatoes and slice them very evenly and thinly. This is best done on a *mandoline* cutter. Put the slices in a large bowl and add salt, pepper and nutmeg, tossing them to get an even spread of seasoning. Butter a shallow 3 pint/1.7 litre baking dish with half the butter. Spread a layer of potatoes, sprinkle it with cheese. Add another layer of potatoes, then a layer of cheese, and so on. Finish with a slightly thicker layer of cheese. Add the stock (to come about three-quarters way up the dish). Dot the top with the remaining butter.

Put the baking dish in a hot oven at 400°F/200°C/Gas Mark 6 for 10 minutes. Reduce the oven temperature to 325°F/160°C/Gas Mark 3 and continue to cook for about 45 minutes until the potatoes are tender when prodded with a fork, the stock has evaporated and the top is nicely browned. If the stock seems to dry up too quickly (depending on the potatoes used), add a little more.

SPRING ROLLS WITH A PEANUT SAUCE
Serves Four

Fresh spring rolls quite surprise by their intensity of flavour, a wonderful follow up to a simple main course.

2 oz/50g Chinese leaf
2 oz/50g carrots

Spring Rolls with a Peanut Sauce

2 oz/50g spring onions
1 clove garlic
1 teaspoon chopped fresh ginger root
1 tablespoon sesame oil
1 tablespoon vegetable oil
2 oz/50g bamboo shoots, chopped
4 oz/125g beansprouts
2 tablespoons *miso* — soya paste
16 spring roll wrappers, available from Chinese
    food stores
1 teaspoon cornflour mixed with 1 tablespoon cold
    water
vegetable oil for frying
For the peanut sauce
4 oz/125g peanuts
1 tablespoon sesame oil
1 tablespoon vegetable oil
1 clove garlic, peeled and chopped
2 teaspoons grated fresh ginger root
4 fl oz/120ml chicken stock
1 teaspoon *miso*
1 tablespoon honey

First make the sauce. Roast the peanuts in an oven preheated to 400°F/200°C/Gas Mark 6 for about 4 minutes. Rub the nuts between the palms of your hands to remove their skins. Heat the oils in a frying pan. Add the nuts and fry over low heat with the chopped garlic and ginger for 3 minutes. Tip the contents of the frying pan into a blender. Add the stock, *miso* and honey and blend to a purée. Add more stock, if necessary: the sauce should be smooth and thick but not too stiff.

Prepare and finely slice the Chinese leaf, carrots and spring onions; peel and chop the garlic.

Heat the oils in a wok or large frying pan. Add the garlic and ginger and fry for 30 seconds. Turn up the heat, add the carrots and fry for 1 minute. Add the spring onions and fry for 30 seconds. Add the Chinese leaf and bamboo shoots, and fry for 30 seconds. Add the beansprouts and fry for 30 seconds more. Add the *miso* and 1 tablespoon water and toss well.

Lay the wrappers on the table. Place a spoonful

of the vegetable mixture across the centre, fold two sides in then roll up as if a pancake. Brush the last edge with the cornflour and water mixture to make it stick.

Heat some oil in a wok or frying pan. Add the spring rolls and fry over medium high heat, turning regularly, until they are golden brown.

Reheat the sauce and serve with the spring rolls.

PLUM TART FROM ALSACE
Serves Six
Alsace is the home of goose liver pâté, wonderful wines, *eaux de vie* and plums. This makes a large tart, in a 12 inch/30cm case, which is well worth the effort.
1 lb/450g shortcrust pastry
2 lb/900g plums
10 oz/275g sugar
4 eggs
5 oz/150g flour
5 fl oz/150ml milk or single cream
2 fl oz/50ml plum brandy
icing sugar for sprinkling

Have the pastry well chilled. Roll it out thinly to line a 12 inch/30cm tart case (preferably with a removable bottom). Press it tight into the corners and prick the base all over with a fork. Line the pastry with foil or greaseproof paper. Weigh down with dried beans and bake for 12 minutes in a preheated oven at 425°F/220°C/Gas Mark 7. Remove the foil and beans and dry out the pastry for another minute or so, if necessary — it should be a light gold.

Halve the plums and remove the stones. Cook in a covered saucepan with 6 ounces/175g of the sugar and 1 tablespoon water over medium heat for about 15 minutes until tender. Remove the plums with a slotted spoon and place them over the pastry base.

Make the filling by beating the eggs with the remaining sugar. Add the flour and continue to beat while adding the milk or cream and the brandy. Pour over the plums. Bake in the oven at 400°F/200°C/Gas Mark 6 for about 25 minutes

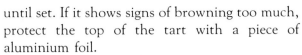

until set. If it shows signs of browning too much, protect the top of the tart with a piece of aluminium foil.

Sprinkle the tart with icing sugar and serve it hot or at room temperature.

CARAMEL MERINGUE
Serves Four

A simple Portuguese recipe. I have suggested a thin custard to accompany it but cream is as nice and the pudding goes well with soft fruit. However, by using custard you will consume all the eggs in one tidy session.

6 oz/175g sugar
3 egg whites
1 tablespoon flaked toasted almonds

For the custard sauce
9 fl oz/275ml milk
1 oz/25g vanilla sugar
3 egg yolks

Put 4 oz/125g of the sugar and 4 tablespoons water in a small heavy pan over low heat. When the sugar has dissolved boil to a rich caramel colour. Add 4 more tablespoons of water (tilt the pan away from you to avoid splashes and burns) and stir until smooth. Reserve.

Whisk the egg whites to soft peaks, fold in the remaining sugar and continue beating. Reheat the caramel to boiling and pour it onto the meringue in a thin stream, whisking all the time. Do not stop until it is thick. Put into a bowl and chill. Scatter with almonds and serve with the custard sauce.

To make the sauce, heat the milk with the vanilla sugar. Pour onto the egg yolks in a bowl, stirring as you do it. Strain into a double boiler set over simmering water. Cook until it just coats the back of the spoon, stirring often. Cool before serving.

COCONUT CUSTARD
Serves Four

This dish is cooked in Sri Lanka and, especially, Malaysia, an unexpected form of baked egg custard. You can use canned coconut milk diluted with water to the given quantity, or desiccated coconut — 8 ounces/225g soaked in 1 pint/600ml hot milk for 30 minutes then pushed through a fine strainer or muslin.

1 coconut
1 pint/600ml plus 3 fl oz/85ml water
4 oz/125g brown sugar
4 eggs
1 tablespoon rosewater
pinch ground mace

Open the coconut by holding it over the sink and giving it a sharp crack with the blunt side of a cleaver. It should break in two. Discard the water. Using a sharp knife cut out the flesh. If this proves difficult put the coconut halves in a moderate oven for 15 to 20 minutes or until the shells crack. Prise out the flesh, peel away the brown skin and cut into chunks. Put the chunks into a blender with ½ pint/300ml of the water. Blend for 1 minute. Pour into a sieve and press out as much liquid as you can get. Return the pulp to the blender and add the other ½ pint/300ml water. Repeat the sieving. Discard the pulp, reserve the milk.

Dissolve the sugar in 3 fluid ounces/85ml water in a pan to make a syrup. In a bowl, combine the eggs, the sugar syrup, rosewater, mace and coconut milk. Strain into a pie dish. Cover with greaseproof paper. Stand the pie dish in a shallow baking dish. Pour in enough hot water to come two-thirds up the sides of the pie dish. Put the baking dish in the oven preheated to 300°F/150°C/Gas Mark 2 for about an hour or until set. Serve cold.

SCORPIO

SUN IN SCORPIO 24 OCTOBER - 22 NOVEMBER
RULED BY MARS

SCORPIO is a cold, moist, fixed, water sign, a combination which denotes the most intense emotions and one of the strongest personalities in the Zodiac. A love of the truth means that people born under this sign are likely to be concerned about the real nature of the food they eat, and especially alert to the perils of suspicious chemical additives. They are likely to fall into fussy eating habits, which they later find difficult to change.

SCORPIO ENVIRONMENTS
Scorpio rules gardens, orchards, vineyards, all places near water and underground habitats. Scorpios adore dark mysterious environments, and usually prefer peace and quiet to noise, although many relish the noise of a dark underground discotheque, at least for a short time. The intimate corner of a cellar bar is an ideal retreat, especially if there is a fountain playing nearby. The light from a single candle is sufficient to excite the deep Scorpionic imagination. In the home, Scorpio rules the larder and kitchen as a whole. In the kitchen it rules the sink.

SCORPIO FOODS
As a water sign Scorpio rules all aquatic animals, including frogs and snails. It is also associated with fermented foods such as the fish sauce and shrimp paste, which are staples in Southeast Asia, or well hung meat such as some game birds. Foods ruled by Mars are also associated with Scorpio.

SHRIMP REMOULADE
Serves Four
Inspired by the cooking of New Orleans, this spicy salad makes a fine start to a meal. Serve it on a bed of shredded lettuce.

1 bay leaf, 1 dried chilli, ½ teaspoon each of coriander seed, mustard seed and allspice tied in a muslin bag
4 pints/2.3 litres water
3 teaspoons salt
1 lb/450g fresh uncooked prawns in their shells, washed
1 spring onion
1 stick celery
½ bunch parsley
8 tablespoons lemon mayonnaise
2 teaspoons Dijon mustard
2 tablespoons single cream
¼ teaspoon cayenne pepper

In a saucepan boil the spice bag in salted water for 5 minutes. Add the prawns and boil, uncovered, for about 2 minutes — they will turn pink. Drain the prawns and refresh by tipping them into a large bowl of iced water; discard the spice bag. Take any eggs off the prawns and reserve in a mortar.

Cut the spring onion and celery into extremely fine slices. Chop the parsley. Pound the prawn eggs in a mortar. Stir them into the mayonnaise with the rest of the ingredients except the prawns themselves. Drain the prawns. Serve them shelled or unshelled, with the sauce in separate bowls.

SEAFOOD GUMBO
Serves Six
This substantial and spicy soup is almost a one-pot meal in itself. Spoon it into shallow soup plates over some boiled rice.

8 oz/225g fresh or frozen prawns in their shells
2 pints/1.1 litres water
6 oysters
1 lb/450g mussels
2 onions
2 cloves garlic

1 red pepper
1 lb/450g okra
14 oz/400g can tomatoes
2 oz/50g butter
bouquet garni of bay leaf, thyme and parsley
salt
½ teaspoon cayenne pepper
6 oz/175g cooked crab meat
2 tablespoons chopped parsley

Shell and devein the prawns and set aside. Boil the shells in the water for 20 minutes. Strain and reserve the stock.

Open the oysters, reserve the flesh and strain their liquor into the prawn stock.

Clean the mussels. Put them in a large covered pan with 2 tablespoons water and cook for 5 to 8 minutes or until they open. Remove the mussels from their shells and reserve. Strain the cooking liquor into the prawn stock. Measure the stock and make it up to 2½ pints/1.4 litres with water. Reserve.

Peel and chop the onions and garlic; seed and chop the pepper; top, tail and thinly slice the okra; chop the tomatoes roughly. Melt the butter in a pan and fry the onion, garlic and pepper over high heat for 5 minutes, stirring to avoid burning. Add the okra and continue cooking for 5 minutes. Add the tomatoes, *bouquet garni*, salt, cayenne and the prawn stock. Turn down the heat and simmer, covered, for 1 hour. Add the osyters, mussels and prawns and cook for 3 minutes. Stir in the crab meat. Check the seasoning. Sprinkle the parsley on top. Serve hot.

GRAVLAKS
This recipe is best done with a whole fish, either salmon or salmon trout. If the fish is smaller use proportionately less of the ingredients listed below. For this dish, too, the fish must be frozen for at least 24 hours before using.

Serve gravlaks with crispbread, a mustardy sauce or a potato salad.

1 salmon, about 5 lb/2.3kg
4 tablespoons sea salt

2 tablespoons sugar
2 teaspoons mixed white and black pepper, ground
3 fl oz/85ml brandy
1 bunch dill, chopped
Mustard sauce
3 tablespoons Dijon mustard
1 teaspoon mustard powder
2 teaspoons caster sugar
2 tablespoons wine vinegar
5 tablespoons vegetable oil
1 bunch chopped dill
black pepper

Defrost the salmon then trim, gut and fillet. Mix together the sea salt, sugar and peppers. Place one fillet skin side down on a china dish. Sprinkle it with the brandy, then half the mixed ingredients and lastly the dill. Rub the other fillet with the remaining dry ingredients, then lay it on top, head to tail, skin side up. Cover with aluminium foil. Put a board on top of the fish with a 4 pound/1.8kg weight on top. Leave in the cool at 40°F/5°C for 3 days. Change the fillets round every 12 hours. basting them with their juices as you do so.

To make the sauce, whisk all the ingredients together in the given order.

Scrape off the dill and cut the fillets thinly, as you would smoked salmon. Serve with the sauce.

GUINEA FOWL WITH GREEN PEPPERCORNS
Serves Four
2 guinea fowl, dressed weight about 2 lb/900g each
2 tablespoons green peppercorns
6 oz/175g butter
a squeeze of lemon
salt and pepper
6 fl oz/175ml white wine
6 fl oz/175ml well reduced guinea fowl stock, made
  with the giblets (not the livers)
6 fl oz/175ml double cream

Truss the fowl for roasting.

Crush the green peppercorns with the back of a spoon. Set one-half aside. Knead the rest into half the butter with a squeeze of lemon juice.

Make a slit at the junction of wings to breasts and spread this peppercorn butter over the flesh and under the skin of the breasts. Season the guinea fowl and place in a roasting pan with the rest of the butter. Roast in a preheated oven at 450°F/230°C Gas Mark 8 for about 25 minutes, basting frequently. When done, lift out the birds and set aside in a warm place while the sauce is finished in the pan.

Pour off the excess fat. Put the roasting pan over heat and add the white wine, scraping the bottom and sides of the pan to amalgamate all the sediment and juices. Boil vigorously to reduce by three-quarters. Then pour in the reduced stock and the remainder of the peppercorns and continue boiling to reduce by half. Add the cream and return to the boil until the sauce is glossy and unctuous. Check for seasoning then pour round the birds on their serving dish.

PHEASANT WITH NORWEGIAN CHEESE
Serves Six
This continues the game theme apposite to Scorpio, a sign that also loves blue cheese. This Norwegian *gjetost* — a caramelized whey cheese made from boiled down goat's milk — is not blue, but its strangely sweet flavour marries well with game. Instead of pheasant, you could use guinea fowl or any rarer game bird, the Norwegians cook ptarmigan this way. Serve with a currant jelly or a dish of cranberries, and rice. French beans might be good afterwards.
4 oz/125g bacon
2 oz/50g butter
2 pheasant, trimmed and trussed
10 fl oz/300ml single cream
5 fl oz/150ml sour cream
2-4 oz/50-125g *gjetost* (according to taste), thinly
  sliced
salt and black pepper
watercress for decoration

Remove the rind and cut the bacon into small pieces. In a casserole big enough to hold the pheasant closely, fry the bacon in the butter until

Gravlaks

the fat runs. Add the pheasant and brown all over. Pack the birds neatly in the casserole with the breasts downwards. Pour in the single cream to a depth of about ½ inch/1 cm, adding water, if necessary, and bring to the boil. Cover the casserole and cook in a preheated oven at 350°F/180°C/Gas Mark 4 for about 1 hour, turning the pheasant over after 30 minutes. They may take longer, depending on age and size.

Remove the birds to a covered dish and keep warm while you finish the sauce. Put the casserole over heat and boil to reduce the cooking liquid to a sauce consistency. Add the sour cream and thin slices of the *gjetost*. Stir until the cheese has melted and the sauce is smooth. Taste for seasoning, then add salt and black pepper. Pour the sauce round the birds, and garnish with a lot of watercress.

OYSTERS ROCKEFELLER
Serves Four
This Scorpionic dish is rich, too rich for some people as a main course, in which case, serve it as a first course. Serve with salads, perhaps one of cucumber and some leeks with lemon and sugar and, of course, brown bread and butter.

36 Pacific oysters
4 spring onions
2 sticks celery
1 lb/450g spinach
4 oz/125g butter
4 tablespoons chopped parsley
3 fl oz/85 ml single cream
1 teaspoon anchovy sauce
10 drops Tabasco
2 tablespoons Pernod
rock salt

Open the oysters. Reserve the flesh. Strain the liquor through muslin and reserve. Scrub the bottom shells and reserve. Chop the spring onions and celery. Wash the spinach, strip away any large ribs and drain well.

Melt the butter in a large saucepan. Add the onions and celery and fry, without browning, for 3 minutes. Add the spinach, cover and cook, stirring occasionally for 5 minutes. Tip the contents of the pan into a blender, with the parsley, cream, anchovy sauce, Tabasco and Pernod. Blend to a purée. Add seasoning, but take into account the saltiness of the oysters.

Lay a bed of rock salt about ½ inch/1 cm deep in 4 shallow oven pans. Arrange the oyster half-shells on the salt settling them in so they stand firm. Put an oyster, a teaspoon of oyster liquor and a spoonful of the purée into each shell. Bake in a preheated oven at 450°F/230°C/ Gas Mark 8 for 4 minutes. Serve hot, in the pans.

A BLUE CHEESE SALAD
Serves Four
The chicory seems a suitable salad plant for Scorpio and because of the sign's coldness, salads rather than hot vegetables should be the order of the day. This very simple affair has the cheese crumbled into the salad itself. However, you could equally well blend it into the dressing, like an American blue cheese dressing.
2 heads *radicchio* (red leafed chicory)
1 small cos lettuce
½ red pepper

2 oz/50g walnuts
4 oz/125g blue cheese, Roquefort or Stilton
For the dressing
1 tablespoon walnut oil
3 tablespoons olive oil
1 tablespoon wine vinegar
salt and black pepper

Wash the chicory and lettuce. Strip the leaves into a bowl (halving the cos leaves if too big).

Cut the red pepper into small dice. Break the walnuts into small pieces. Crumble the blue cheese. Add all to the lettuce and mix lightly. Make the dressing and toss the salad 10 minutes before serving.

CUCUMBER SALAD
Serves Four to Six
In Scandinavia this is called 'fresh pickled' and it has many Scorpio characteristics, not least the need to marinate to bring about the combination of flavours. Cucumber salad is often served with hot meals as well as fish dishes and is also used as a sandwich filling.
1 cucumber
1 bunch dill
2 tablespoons soft brown sugar
4 fl oz/120ml wine vinegar
½ teaspoon salt
½ teaspoon black pepper

Wipe the cucumber and slice it thinly. Chop the dill. Mix the sugar, vinegar, 2 tablespoons of water, salt and pepper well together to make a dressing. Arrange the cucumber in a shallow dish and pour on the dressing. Leave to marinate for 3 hours. Lift out the cucumber slices and place them on another dish. Sprinkle generously with dill.

VEGETABLES WITH LEMON AND OIL
Serves Six
This method of cooking vegetables is especially Greek, but it is common throughout the Levant. The long marinating is also right for Scorpionic foods. And some of the vegetables, onions and

leeks especially, are Martian in character. You may use many different kinds of vegetables in this way, serving eight or more at one time. The cold-wet aspect of the sign is of course well covered by the nature of this recipe. It can be eaten as a first course, as a meal in itself on a hot day, or can even be served warm, as a more elaborate foil to a plain meat or fish course.

8 fl oz/250ml white wine
2 pints/1.1 litres water
8 fl oz/250ml olive oil
4 fl oz/120ml lemon juice
1 teaspoon salt
2 cloves garlic, peeled
1 stick celery
bouquet garni of parsley, fennel and thyme
1 teaspoon peppercorns
1 teaspoon coriander seeds
16 pickling onions
4-6 leeks
8 oz/225g French beans
16 small carrots

Combine in a large saucepan all the ingredients except the onions, leeks, beans and carrots. Bring to the boil and simmer, covered, for 1 hour. Strain the stock and return it to the pan.

Prepare the vegetables: peel the onions; wash and trim the leeks; top and tail the beans; scrub the carrots, cut off their tails but leave the bottoms of their stalks. In the uncovered pan, cook each vegetable in turn in the stock until tender. Using a slotted spoon, transfer them onto a dish.

When they are all cooked, boil the stock until it is reduced to one cupful. Strain the stock over the vegetables and leave to cool for 12 hours.

BEANS WITH SAFFRON, TOMATO AND EGG
Serves Four

This dish combines some of the characteristics of Martian foods with the moistness of Scorpio. Serve it hot or cool, as a substantial vegetable accompaniment or on its own. A bowl of plain yoghurt is good with it.

12 oz/350g dried white beans
2 onions
2 cloves garlic
a generous pinch (or 1 sachet) saffron threads
5 fl oz/150ml olive oil
1 tablespoon tomato purée
1 bunch parsley, chopped
salt and black pepper
3 eggs

Soak the beans overnight in cold water. Peel and slice 1 onion and the garlic. Peel and chop the other onion. Drain the beans and put them to boil with the sliced onion and garlic in an uncovered saucepan with enough water to cover. Boil for 10 minutes. Then simmer covered for 1 to 2 hours (depending on the age of the beans) until tender. Add a little more water if the pan shows signs of drying out.

Meanwhile, soak the saffron threads in 1 tablespoon warm water for 15 minutes. Heat the olive oil in a large frying pan. Add the chopped onion and fry until golden brown. Add the tomato purée, saffron and its soaking water, chopped parsley and lots of black pepper and heat through. Add the beans and any remaining cooking water and continue to cook until all the liquid has been absorbed. Season carefully with salt.

Break the eggs into a bowl and beat lightly. Stir them into the beans over very low heat and cook until the eggs have just started to bind.

LITTLE MOCHA CREAMS
Serves Four

Vienna, the home of the finest pastries, desserts and luxurious sweets, is an apt inspiration for this simplest and most toothsome of all chocolate creams. The addition of coffee gives it some bite. The chocolate must be bitter and of good quality. It really needs nothing with it, except perhaps an almond biscuit.

½ vanilla pod or 3 drops vanilla essence
10 fl oz/300ml single cream
2 teaspoons instant coffee
pinch salt

7 oz/200g bitter chocolate
1 egg

Scrape the seeds from the vanilla pod into the cream in a small saucepan. Put the pod itself into the pan as well. Bring the cream just up to the boil. Remove the pod. Add the coffee and stir to dissolve. Add the salt.

Break the chocolate into bits and put in a blender. Pour on the scalded cream and blend until smooth. Add the egg and blend again. Pour into small dishes, one per person. Chill and serve.

APPLES FLAMED WITH CALVADOS
Serves Four
8 small Cox's Orange Pippin apples
2 oz/50g unsalted butter
2 oz/50g sugar
juice of ½ lemon
juice of ½ orange
1½ fl oz/40ml Calvados
whipped cream for serving

Peel, quarter and core the apples. Cut into thin slices. Melt the butter with the sugar in a deep sauté pan. Add the apples and cook gently for about 4 minutes, shaking the pan, until nearly tender. Add the juice of the lemon and orange, boil fast to reduce. Warm the Calvados, set it alight and pour over the apples. Serve immediately with the cream.

EMPEROR'S OMELETTE
Serves Two
A strikingly simple idea for a sweet dish from Vienna, balanced by the tartness of stewed plums or other sharp red fruit (to keep within Mars's requirements) that you serve with it. Cranberries are very good; the Austrians have a thing about their small black plums, but you could also use rhubarb (an apt food for Scorpio). This recipe is enough to fill one medium-sized frying pan. The mixture should be about 1 inch/2.5cm deep in the pan.
3 oz/75g flour
pinch salt
2 tablespoons caster sugar

6 fl oz/175ml milk
1 oz/25g sultanas
1 oz/25g butter plus a knob for the pan
2 eggs
cranberries
cream for serving

In a bowl mix together the flour, salt, 1 tablespoon of the sugar, the milk and sultanas. Beat well. Melt the butter and beat it in. Separate the eggs and add the yolks to the batter. Whisk the whites to firm peaks and fold them in.

Melt a knob of butter in the pan over medium heat. Pour in the batter and cook until one side is golden brown. Turn and cook the other side.

Take two forks and tear the omelette apart into little strips or pieces, while still in the pan but off the heat. Return to the heat and continue to fry until they have crisped. Dredge with sugar and serve with cranberries.

NORWEGIAN PRUNE PUDDING
Serves Four
This recipe has something of Scorpio about it: it is cold and moist, has the long-keeping attributes associated with prunes, as well as their laxative qualities (a Martian characteristic). Serve it cold, of course, with cream.
24 jumbo prunes, soaked and cooked
10 fl oz/300ml water
1 inch/2.5cm stick cinnamon
6 oz/175g sugar
2 oz/50g cornflour
10 fl oz/300ml single cream plus extra for serving
1 tablespoon lemon juice

Stone the prunes. Put the prune pulp in a saucepan with the water, cinnamon stick and sugar. Cook, uncovered, for 10 minutes. Mix the cornflour in a little water and add to the pan, stirring until the liquid thickens. Remove the cinnamon. Stir in the single cream and the lemon juice, continue to cook until thick and smooth.

Rinse a mould or bowl with cold water and leave wet. Pour in the prune mixture and leave to cool in the refrigerator. Turn out when set and serve.

SAGITTARIUS

SUN IN SAGITTARIUS 23 NOVEMBER - 21 DECEMBER
RULED BY JUPITER

SAGITTARIUS is the restless wanderer of the Zodiac, and people born under this sign are famous for their tendency to change course in midstream. They prize their personal freedom above all else, and their search for liberation often results in long and adventurous journeys of exploration; they also have a pronounced philosophical bent, and are just as likely to set off on journeys of inner liberation. They are, in general, civilized people and in the eleventh century the Arabs noted that they were 'particular as to food and drink'. Sagittarius is a hot, dry, masculine fire sign.

SAGITTARIUS ENVIRONMENTS

Highlands, hills, orchards, stables, rooms at the top of houses and firesides have all been noted as typical Sagittarian places. This suggests that the true Sagittarian prefers to have the dining room at the top of the house, or at least on the first floor, and when eating out will choose a restaurant with a view or on top of a tall building. An open fire is necessary for the ideal meal. A lively atmosphere is preferred, especially somewhere busy where comings and goings can be observed. Airports and all places where people set out on long journeys are Sagittarian.

SAGITTARIUS FOOD

Sagittarius has affinity with birds. It also rules fruits and seeds in general as well as beetroot, onions, radish, comfrey, garlic, saffron, turmeric and vervain. As the ruler of air travel, it is associated with food served on aircraft. In many ways such food satisfies the Sagittarians' impatience and desire to eat quickly or perform some other activity while eating. This is a hot, dry sign, so food which is grilled, toasted, baked or barbecued is appropriate; and quick methods of preparation are preferred. Other foods associated with Sagittarius are those ruled by Jupiter, the sign's ruling planet.

SEA URCHIN OMELETTE
Serves One

Sea Urchins can be found in markets of the northern hemisphere, as well as in the Pacific. They can also be bought in tins, exported from Japan. They make an omelette with a difference. A rich beginning to a meal, as is decreed by Jupiter's protection — a planet of rich and lavish eating.

4 sea urchins
2 eggs
black pepper
1 oz/25g butter

Open the sea urchins and reserve their coral flesh. Strain their liquor through a muslin and reserve 1 tablespoonful. Beat the eggs with a fork with the liquor and seasoning. Add the corals.

Melt the butter over medium high heat in an 8 inch/20 cm omelette pan until hot but not quite smoking. Pour the omelette mixture into the pan to cover the bottom. Stir the mixture with the back of the fork for 20 seconds. Turn down the heat to medium. Pull back the edges of the omelette to allow the uncooked runny mixture to come in contact with the heat. When it is sufficiently cooked, and an omelette should still be creamy inside — not entirely set — fold it in half and tip out of the pan onto a warmed plate.

AUBERGINE PUREE WITH CHILLI
Serves Four

An Eastern European treatment of a dish that is popular in the Mediterranean region. The pimento and chilli as well as the grilling of the aubergine remind us of the Jupiter/Sagittarian preference for hot/dry methods of cooking. Eat this with flat bread, or toasted French bread, some very young and mild spring onions and a dish of yoghurt seasoned with salt and pepper.

1 large aubergine
2 cloves garlic
juice of 1 lemon
4 tablespoons olive oil
salt
1 large green pepper

1 hot red chilli
2 large tomatoes
1 bunch parsley
paprika

Prick the aubergine quite deeply all over with a fork. Put it on a rack under a medium high grill. Grill for 20 to 30 minutes, turning regularly, until the skin is all blistered and charred. (It is also possible to roast the aubergine in a hot oven, or to grill it over charcoal.)

Scrape the skin and burnt bits off the aubergine. Put the flesh in a bowl and mash to a pulp. Peel and crush the garlic and mix in along with the lemon juice. Beat in the oil slowly. Season with salt.

Halve and seed the green pepper and red chilli and chop very fine; skin, seed and chop the tomatoes very fine; wash and chop the parsley. Stir the pepper, chilli, tomato and half the parsley into the aubergine. Turn onto a dish and leave to cool for an hour.

Serve with the rest of the parsley and a scattering of paprika sprinkled over the top.

TOMATO, ORANGE AND CARDAMOM SOUP
Serves Four

This recipe draws on some of the ingredients of Sagittarius' fellow fire signs, Aries and Leo, to create a truly Sagittarian mix.

1 onion
1 carrot
1 potato
3 lb/1.4kg ripe tomatoes
3 oz/75g butter
zest of ½ orange
seeds from 4 cardamom pods, crushed
10-15 fl oz/300-450ml chicken stock
salt and black pepper
sugar
4 fl oz/120ml double cream

Peel and slice the onion and carrot; peel and dice the potato; chop the tomatoes roughly. Melt the butter in a saucepan and fry the onion until tender but not brown. Add the carrot, potato, tomatoes, orange zest and cardamom to the saucepan. Cook, uncovered, for 25 minutes.

Purée the vegetables through the fine plate of a food mill and return to the saucepan. Add the stock and bring to the boil. Cook for 2 minutes. Add salt and pepper and, if necessary, sugar. Stir in the cream and serve.

GRILLED TUSCAN SQUAB
Serves Four

The hills of Tuscany, washed by the setting sun into stripes of gold and black shadow, is the place for simple grilled foods over a wood or charcoal fire. Squab are favoured by Sagittarius and eat better too, though very young and tender wood pigeons will have more flavour and still grill satisfactorily. Eat with buttered rice and a dish of mixed mushrooms and dried *porcini* (cep) from Italy, stewed in butter.

4 squab or young pigeons
1 carrot
1 small leek
1 stick celery
4 fl oz/120ml olive oil
¾-1 pint/450-600ml cold water
2 sprigs marjoram
juice of 1 lemon
1 tablespoon chopped parsley
grated rind of ½ lemon
salt and black pepper
4 oz/125g butter

Gut the birds and split them in half through the back so they are spread out like butterflies. Reserving the livers, use the rest of the giblets for the stock.

To make the stock, clean and slice the carrot, leek and celery. Heat 1 fluid ounce/25ml of the olive oil in a saucepan. Add the vegetables and fry until browned. Add the water, the giblets and marjoram. Boil, uncovered, for 30 minutes. Strain the stock and reserve.

Make a marinade with the lemon juice, the remaining olive oil, parsley and lemon rind. Season the birds and pour the marinade over them,

turning to coat them well. Cover and leave in the refrigerator for 30 minutes.

Lift the birds out of the marinade, place on a rack in the grilling pan and grill under medium heat for 7 to 15 minutes on each side, depending on size. Brush with the marinade regularly. When cooked, keep them warm while you finish making the sauce.

Chop the livers. Heat half the butter in a saucepan and fry the chopped liver for 30 seconds. Add the juices from the grilling pan and the stock. Boil hard to reduce the liquid to a few spoonfuls of strong tasting broth. Whisk in the rest of the butter, a little at a time, and check the seasoning.

To serve, transfer the birds to warmed plates and pour the sauce over them.

CATALAN CHICKEN
Serves Four to Six

This braised chicken is typical of many Catalan dishes, even if it does not include the chilli so beloved of their kitchens. Serve this with no more than a green salad and some rice. A separate dish of broad beans could be offered afterwards.

1 chicken, about 3½ lb/1.6kg
salt
4 large onions
6 large cooking tomatoes
2 green peppers
2 aubergines
9 fl oz/275ml olive oil

Wipe the chicken, cut into four and rub with salt. Peel and chop the onions; skin, seed and chop the tomatoes; seed and slice the peppers. Slice the aubergines and put them in a colander with a dusting of salt. Leave to drain for 30 minutes under a weighted plate.

In a large casserole, fry half the onions in 3 fluid ounces/85ml of the olive oil until well browned. Add half the tomatoes and cook, uncovered, for 5 minutes. Add the chicken pieces and simmer, covered, for 30 minutes. Turn and baste regularly.

Meanwhile, in another pan, fry the rest of the onion in 3 fluid ounces/85ml of the olive oil until slightly browned. Add the sliced peppers and fry for about 5 minutes until nearly tender. Add the rest of the tomatoes and cook for 5 minutes more.

In a third pan, heat the rest of the olive oil. Add the aubergine slices and fry, a few at a time, over fairly high heat, browning them on both sides. Drain on kitchen paper before adding them to the onions and peppers.

Add the onion, pepper and aubergine mixture to the casserole and cook, covered, for a further 15 minutes, over a very low heat, until the chicken is thoroughly cooked.

Hungarian Platter Steak

HUNGARIAN PLATTER STEAK
Serves Four

Small wonder that Sagittarius, half horse, half man, is associated with the Huns and Mongols who swept out of the Asian steppes in the Dark Ages, spreading mayhem and panic before settling on the vast plains of Eastern Europe. To these warriors on the move, the grill was the natural cooking technique and the platter steak, a form of mixed grill served on a wooden platter, is the modern equivalent. This is a substantial dish, served usually with sauté potatoes, mixed pickles

and pepper or cabbage salads, but you could offer some Potatoes Paprikash (*see* below).

3 onions
6 tomatoes
4 oz/125g lard
1 tablespoon paprika
1 tablespoon chopped marjoram
salt and pepper
8 thin slices beef fillet, each about 2 oz/50g
1 tablespoon Dijon mustard
4 thin slices pork tenderloin, each about 1½ oz/40g
4 thin rashers streaky bacon
4 thin slices calf's liver, each about 2-3 oz/50-75g
4 slices veal fillet, each about 2 oz/50g

Peel and slice the onions; skin, seed and coarsely chop the tomatoes. Heat half the lard in a frying pan. Add the onions and fry until golden. Stir in the paprika. Add the tomatoes and cook for 5 minutes. Add the marjoram and salt and pepper. Keep hot.

Season the beef fillet and spread one side of each slice with mustard. Season the pork fillet. Take the rind off the bacon. Cut the rashers in half and stretch them with the back of a knife. Make 4 sandwiches: the beef on the outside (mustard facing in) with the pork and bacon as filling. Keep them together with cocktail sticks. Season the liver and veal fillet.

Grill all the meats under high heat, brushing with the remaining lard. The beef sandwich will need longer cooking, so that the pork is cooked through, about 5 to 8 minutes on each side. The liver and veal should be cooked pink, 2 to 3 minutes each side.

Serve on wooden platters, if you have them, with the onion and tomato mixture and any of the suggested accompaniments.

POTATOES PAPRIKASH
Serves Four
A sustaining dish that need not include the sausage if you want to serve it as an accompaniment, or would rather not eat meat.

1 onion
1 clove garlic
½ green pepper
2 lb/900g potatoes
4 oz/125g lard
½ teaspoon chilli powder
1 tablespoon paprika
¼ teaspoon ground caraway
1 teaspoon tomato purée
salt
6 oz/175g smoked sausage or Frankfurters

Peel and chop the onion; peel and chop the garlic; dice the green pepper; peel and cut the potatoes into small cubes.

Heat the lard in a heavy pan and fry the onion until golden. Add the garlic and the green pepper. Continue frying over low heat for 3 minutes. Add the spices, tomato purée and salt and fry for a further 2 minutes. Add the potatoes. Cover the pan and cook over low heat, stirring occasionally, for 15 minutes. Barely cover with water, bring to the boil and cook very gently, uncovered, for 15 to 20 minutes until the potatoes are soft. Ten minutes before the end, cut the sausage in thick slices and then add to the pan. The consistency should be of a very thick soup rather than completely dry.

MAGYAR MUSHROOMS
Serves Four
An excellent way with mushrooms, cooked with sour cream, the preferred cream for culinary use in Eastern Europe. If you use dried ceps or *porcini*, usually available from delicatessens, don't forget to save the water in which you soak them for some other use. It has a marvellous mushroom flavour. In Hungary, they often serve these mushrooms with fried eggs.

1 packet dried ceps, about ¾ oz/20g
2 onions
1½ lb/700g button mushrooms
3 oz/75g butter
salt and black pepper
10 fl oz/300ml sour cream

2 teaspoons paprika
1 tablespoon parsley
lemon juice, if necessary

Soak the ceps in tepid water for 30 minutes; peel and chop the onions; wipe (don't wash) the mushrooms. Heat the butter in a frying pan and fry the onions for about 10 minutes or until golden. Add the mushrooms. Drain the ceps and add them, too. Season with salt and pepper. Cook, covered, stirring occasionally, for 10 minutes, then uncovered, stirring often, for another 5 to 10 minutes until all the liquid has evaporated and the mushrooms are tender.

Add the sour cream, paprika and parsley. Boil fiercely for 2 minutes until the sauce is smooth and thick. Check seasoning, perhaps adding a little lemon juice. Serve hot.

PEAS AND HAM
Serves Four
An Italian custom is to cook garden peas with some cooked ham. It works better with fresh vegetables than with the frozen packets of soft sweet peas. Jupiter, lover of rich foods, would approve stirring in some double cream at the end of cooking.
3 lb/1.4kg fresh peas
1 small onion
2 oz/50g butter
10 fl oz/300ml water
3 oz/75g cooked ham
salt and black pepper

Shell the peas; peel and chop the onion. Heat the butter in a saucepan and fry the onion gently for about 5 minutes until tender. Add the peas and the water. Cook, covered, for about 10 minutes.

Cut the ham into matchsticks and add to the pan 5 minutes before the end. Season last of all, depending on the saltiness of the ham.

ASPARAGUS GRATIN
Serves Four
A Hungarian recipe for dealing with a Jupiter food.
2 lb/900g asparagus
salt

3 oz/75g butter
5 fl oz/150ml sour cream
paprika
4 tablespoons soft breadcrumbs

Prepare the asparagus and peel if necessary. Blanch in boiling salted water for about 5 minutes (less if very small and fresh).

Butter a gratin dish. Drain the asparagus and put in the dish. Pour in the sour cream. Season with salt and paprika. Sprinkle the breadcrumbs over the top. Dot with the remaining butter. Cook in a very hot oven, 450°F/230°C/Gas Mark 8, for about 10 to 15 minutes until browned. Serve at once.

CHEESECAKE
Serves Four to Six
For the pastry
3 oz/75g flour
pinch salt
1 tablespoon sugar
2 oz/50g butter plus extra for the tin
1 egg yolk
For the filling
12 oz/350g curd cheese
3 oz/75g sugar
½ oz/15g semolina
1 egg plus 1 egg yolk
3 fl oz/85ml sour cream
For the topping
1 egg white
1 oz/25g icing sugar
grated rind of ½ lemon

Sift the flour and salt together. Mix in the sugar. Cut in the butter until the mixture resembles crumbs. Mix in the egg yolk with your finger tips, and shape the pastry into a ball. If necessary, add a tablespoon of iced water. Cover the pastry and leave to rest in the cool for 20 minutes.

Butter an 8 inch/20 cm baking tin with fairly deep sides. Roll out the pastry and line the tin with it, pressing it well in. Prick the bottom with a fork. Leave to rest again for 20 minutes.

Meanwhile make the filling. Sieve the curd

cheese into a bowl. Beat in the sugar, semolina, the egg and egg yolk. Beat in the sour cream. Pour into the pastry case and bake in a preheated oven at 400°F/200°C/Gas Mark 6 for 20 to 30 minutes until set and a skewer inserted in the centre comes out clean. Turn off the oven.

To make the topping, whisk the egg white until it forms firm peaks. Fold in the sugar and the grated lemon rind. When the cheesecake comes out of the oven, spread the meringue over the top with a palette knife. Return it to the turned off oven and allow the meringue to dry out in the residual heat for 15 minutes. Serve warm or cool.

TUSCAN CREAM CHEESE WITH SOFT FRUIT
Serves Four

The Italians have wonderful natural cream cheeses; sweetened and enriched, they form a perfect foil for red fruit, or just for eating on their own.

1 pint/600ml double cream
1 teaspoon rennet or 1 rennet tablet dissolved in 2 tablespoons milk
2 oz/50g caster sugar
2 egg yolks
2 tablespoons brandy
ripe loganberries

Heat the double cream to blood heat in a bowl set over simmering water. Stir in the rennet. Stir for 2 minutes. Leave the bowl, covered, at 80°F/27°C for 3 hours by which time it should have set.

Pour the mixture into a clean muslin cloth or nylon jelly bag. Hang it to drain over a bowl for 24 hours, stirring twice during that period. It will then be ready.

Sieve the cream cheese into a bowl. Beat the sugar with the yolks until pale, add the brandy.

Gradually beat the egg mixture into the cheese, continue beating until thick. Chill, and serve with a bowl of very ripe loganberries.

SEED AND SPICE BISCUITS
Makes Twenty

These Spanish biscuits contain many spices favoured by Jupiter and highlight two seeds: sesame and anis. Sagittarius is especially related to seeds. Serve them for tea, with a morning glass of Marsala, or as an accompaniment to coffee at the end of a meal.

10 fl oz/300ml vegetable oil plus extra for the baking sheets
1 tablespoon sesame seed
1 tablespoon aniseed
5 fl oz/150ml white wine
2 teaspoons grated lemon rind
2 teaspoons grated orange rind
2 teaspoons grated fresh ginger root
3 oz/75g sugar
1 lb/450g flour
1 teaspoon ground cinnamon
½ teaspoon ground cloves

Grease 2 baking sheets with a little oil.

Heat the oil in a saucepan. Put in the sesame seed and aniseed. Continue to heat for 1 minute, then leave to cool. Put the seeds and oil into a large bowl and beat in the wine, grated lemon and orange rind, ginger and sugar.

Mix the flour with the spices and add to the rest of the mixture adding a little water if the dough is too dry. Shape the dough into a ball and wrap in clingfilm. Rest for 30 minutes.

Divide the dough into 20 balls. Flatten them onto the greased baking sheets. Bake in a preheated oven at 400°F/200°C/Gas Mark 6 for 15 to 20 minutes. Cool on racks.

CAPRICORN

SUN IN CAPRICORN 22 DECEMBER - 20 JANUARY
RULED BY SATURN

CAPRICORN is a sign of traditional beliefs, down to earth values and material wealth. This is not to say that all Capricorns are rich dyed-in-the-wool conservatives. Far from it: many are artists, others are revolutionaries, living in poverty for their beliefs. Yet, unless they are denying their true natures, they prefer comfort to discomfort and would much rather maintain all that is best about the past than sweep it away. The true Capricorn is fond of food, and will eat almost anything, believing that ultimately the purpose of food is to keep body and soul together. This is a cold, dry, feminine earth sign.

CAPRICORN ENVIRONMENTS

Traditionally Capricorn rules cowsheds, sheep pens and pastures, castles, harbours, places where nautical equipment is stored and lodgings for strangers. Capricorns like eating in restaurants by busy harbours or docksides. There are, however, two kinds of people born under this sign: those who favour a plain traditional environment preferring to eat at home because it is cheaper and who display their frugality in their simply furnished kitchens and dining rooms; and those who enjoy eating in grand old houses and smart restaurants. These Capricorns believe that wealth should be flaunted and will eat out only in those fashionable establishments where they go to see and be seen.

CAPRICORN FOOD

Capricornian food tends typically to be plain rather than rich, although for some it is very important to use food to make a statement about personal success, status and wealth. Lavish dishes from different cuisines are combined for the effect they create rather than for considerations of health or taste. Traditional dishes such as roast lamb and mint sauce or the Thanksgiving turkey have a Capricorn character. This sign rules all self-sowing and propagating plants, herbs and fruits, blackberries, for example, and other wild fruit. Among the meats it rules lamb (also ruled by Aries) together with all herded animals. It is concerned with the bone structure so dishes such as spareribs, or food made from bones, such as gelatine, come under this sign. Other foods associated with this sign are those ruled by Saturn.

BELGIAN MUSSELS
Serves Four

By increasing the quantities you can convert this to a substantial meal, with chips of course if following the Belgian way. Here, it should be eaten as it is, just with bread to mop up the juices.

4 lb/1.8kg mussels
2 small onions
bay leaf
3 fl oz/85ml white wine
1 stick celery
1 bunch parsley
2 gherkins
2 oz/50g butter
1 tablespoon soft breadcrumbs

Wash and clean the mussels; peel and slice 1 of the onions. Set the mussels to boil in a covered pan with the sliced onion, bay leaf and white wine. When they have opened in 5 to 8 minutes, take off the top half of their shells and reserve the mussels in their half shells. Strain the liquor and reserve.

Peel and chop the second onion, chop the celery, parsley and gherkins. Heat the butter in a saucepan and brown the onion and celery. Add the parsley and gherkins. Stir in 1 cup of the strained mussel liquor and the soft breadcrumbs. Cook gently until thickened. Taste for seasoning. Pour over mussels and serve.

ESCOVITCH — ESCABECHE — CAVEACH
Serves Four

The preference of Capricorn for sour and acid foods makes this classic of Spanish, West Indian and Latin American cooking a natural choice. This simple method of pickling fish started in Spain and was carried by the conquistadores to their colonies across the Atlantic. This particular recipe, and the spelling escovitch, comes from Jamaica — originally a Spanish possession though later to become British. Neither olive oil or wine vinegar are Jamaican but both enhance the flavour of the dish. The English version of the word — caveach — is seen often in old recipe books as the recipe had

much popularity in Britain in the 17th and 18th centuries. For a Capricorn meal serve this dish cold rather than hot with brown rolls and butter.

8 mackerel fillets
salt and black pepper
flour for dredging
3 fl oz/85ml olive oil
½ red pepper
½ green pepper
2 onions
1 clove garlic
1 dry chilli
3 slices of lemon
1 bay leaf
10 whole chives
5 fl oz/150ml water
3 fl oz/85ml white wine vinegar
2 teaspoons Angostura bitters

Season the mackerel fillets and dredge them with flour. Fry them on both sides in 2 fluid ounces/50ml of the olive oil for about 4 minutes until just firm. Lay them flat in a dish, skin side down.

Slice the peppers thinly, peel and slice the onions and garlic and chop the chilli. Heat the remaining oil in a saucepan. Add the peppers, onions and garlic and fry for 3 to 5 minutes or until they are just beginning to lose their bite. Add the chilli, the lemon slices, herbs, ½ teaspoon salt and ½ teaspoon black pepper, and the liquids. Bring to the boil and simmer, uncovered, for about 5 minutes, until tender. Pour over the fish, discard the bay leaf and chives, and leave to cool.

GIANT PRAWNS WITH GINGER AND DILL
Serves Four

The ruling planet Saturn favours shellfish and cumin and from the Indian subcontinent comes a very spicy first course that can be offered cool or hot. Saturn has also a leaning towards small portions which may be evinced in this dish too. I have suggested cucumber as a muted accompaniment.

1 cucumber
salt

12 frozen giant Pacific prawns or *crevettes roses*,
  defrosted
1 pint/600ml water
1 inch/2.5cm fresh ginger root
½ fresh green chilli
½ teaspoon ground coriander
½ teaspoon ground cumin
3 tablespoons vegetable oil
salt
juice of ½ lemon
1 bunch dill, chopped
black pepper

Peel, seed and slice the cucumber. Toss the slices
in salt and leave to drain in a colander under a
weighted plate for 20 minutes. Rinse and dry.

Shell and devein the prawns. Put the heads and
shells in a saucepan with the water. Boil to reduce
by half. Strain and reserve the stock.

Pound the ginger and chilli in a mortar with the
ground coriander and cumin. In a saucepan, cook
the spices in the oil until they take colour. Add
the prawns, salt and lemon juice and cook for 1
minute, turning the prawns until coated. Add the
stock and simmer for 1 minute. Taste for seasoning.
Remove the prawns with a slotted spoon to a dish.
Add the dill to the pan and boil to reduce the sauce
by half. Pour over the prawns.

Arrange a bed of cucumber over the bottom of
each plate, season with black pepper, and put the
prawns in the centre.

MEATBALLS WITH YOGHURT AND CARAWAY

Serves Four

The flavouring comes from Yugoslavia and Balkan
countries; the main form — the meatball — was
picked up from the Moors during those centuries
of Turkish occupation. Serve with mashed potato
and buttered broccoli.

1 small onion
oil
1 lb/450g lean lamb for mincing
2 oz/50g soft breadcrumbs
3 fl oz/85ml warm water
1 egg
1 teaspoon salt
black pepper
1 tablespoon brandy
flour for dusting

For the sauce

2 tablespoons flour, mixed in 8 fl oz/250ml water
10 oz/275g natural yoghurt
1 teaspoon caraway seeds, crushed
salt and black pepper

Peel, mince or finely chop the onion. Heat 1
tablespoon oil in a small frying pan and fry the
onion until brown.

Coarsly chop the lamb, put in a food processor
and grind to a fine paste. Mix the crumbs with
the warm water and add to the meat with the egg,
seasoning and brandy. Process very well then add
the onion.

If doing it by hand, put the lamb through a
mincing machine twice. Mix with the other
ingredients, add the onion and beat and knead for
10 minutes.

Shape the mixture into 20 balls and leave to rest
for 10 minutes. Dust or roll the meatballs in flour.
Fry in hot oil for 4 to 6 minutes or until brown
on all sides. Drain on kitchen paper and reserve.

To make the sauce, put the flour and water
mixture and the yoghurt in a saucepan. Mix, then
add the caraway and seasoning. Bring to the boil
and cook very gently, uncovered, for 10 minutes.
Add the meatballs and serve when heated through.

CHICKEN WITH APPLE AND HORSERADISH

Serves Four

This recipe has its origins in the Balkans and
Rumania and is an essay in mixed tastes that recalls
some of the nature of Capricorn. It may be eaten
hot or at room temperature. If eating it hot, serve
some broad beans with it; if cold, perhaps a green
salad of watercress and endives.

1 chicken, about 3 lb/1.4kg
2 onions
2 sticks celery

2 carrots
1 bay leaf
6 peppercorns
For the rice
3 oz/75g leek
2 tablespoons olive oil
6 oz/175g long-grain rice
1 pint/600ml chicken stock
salt and black pepper
For the horseradish sauce
1 tablespoon grated horseradish
5 fl oz/150ml double cream
5 fl oz/150ml chicken stock
salt and pepper
2 egg yolks, beaten
For the apples
4 eating apples
4 oz/125g butter
salt
lemon juice

Truss the chicken for boiling. Peel and halve the onions, prepare and halve the celery and carrots. Put the chicken, giblets (not the liver), vegetables, bay leaf and peppercorns in a saucepan. Pour in enough cold water to cover and bring to the boil. Skim off the fat and scum, then simmer, covered, for about 45 minutes or until tender. Skim twice more during cooking. Take out the chicken and take the flesh off the bone. Discard the skin and carcase. Reserve the flesh.

Meanwhile prepare the rice. Wash the leek and cut into thin rings. Heat the oil in a casserole. Add the leek and fry until transparent. Add the rice and cook for 3 minutes, stirring. Add the stock and seasoning and bring to the boil. Cover the casserole and put in a preheated oven at 250°F/120°C/Gas Mark ½ for about 30 minutes or until the rice is tender and the liquid absorbed.

While the rice is cooking prepare the sauce. Combine the horseradish, cream, stock and salt and pepper in a small pan. Cook for 2 minutes. Remove the pan off the heat and add the egg yolks. Stir the sauce over a very gentle heat, never letting it boil, until it thickens slightly.

Lastly, peel, quarter, core and cut the apples into medium slices. Heat the butter in a pan and fry the apple slices until just softening. Add salt and a little lemon juice. They should not break up.

Arrange the rice on a dish, with the pieces of chicken on top. Pour over the horseradish sauce and put the apples in a line down one side.

BALKAN PORK KEBABS
Serves Four
Allspice is a favourite Balkan flavouring, here combined with the Saturnine meat — pork — and mustard in an easily made kebab. It is quite rich, so a dish of peas cooked with lettuce, onion and chervil might make a soothing partner, together with some fried potatoes.
16 small pickling onions
1 lb/450g trimmed tenderloin of pork, cut in 1 inch/2.5cm cubes
1 teaspoon ground allspice
salt and pepper
1 tablespoon Dijon or German mustard
eggwash made with 1 egg beaten with 4 tablespoons milk
dried breadcrumbs for coating
8 rashers streaky bacon
butter for grilling
Peel the onions. Boil them for 5 minutes in salted water. Drain and reserve.

In a bowl, mix the pork with the allspice, salt and pepper and mustard to coat all over. Dip the pork cubes in the eggwash, then roll in the breadcrumbs. Remove the bacon rind, halve the rashers and roll them up.

Thread the pork, onions and bacon on 4 long skewers. Dribble melted butter over them as you grill them under medium heat for 10 minutes, turning 3 times. Serve hot.

SOUR POTATO SALAD
Serves Four
The Indians have a great range of sour tastes, useful to refresh the palate during or after a rich curry and to counteract the effects of exhaustion from

Balkan Pork Kebabs

the sun and the humidity. This salad is reminiscent of these.

1½ lb/700g of the smallest new potatoes
1 teaspoon cumin seeds
1 tablespoon chopped fresh coriander
juice of ½ lemon
1 tablespoon natural yoghurt
salt and black pepper

Scrub the potatoes. Cook in salted boiling water for 12 minutes or until just tender. Drain and cool.

Put the cumin seeds in a cast iron pan. Dry roast them over high heat for about 2 minutes until they

brown. Cool and grind the cumin in a mortar. Mix with the rest of the ingredients to make a sharp dressing. Toss the cooled potatoes in this.

HOT LIME PICKLE
Makes about two pounds/900g
To continue the sour theme that runs through much of Capricorn/Saturn foods, I have included pickle recipe this for limes (but you can use lemons) from India. To make it satisfactorily you need a stoneware wide-mouthed storage jar or a tall glass jar. The limes are preserved whole, so they need

more space than if they were in slices.
15 limes
10 fresh green chillies
3 oz/75g fresh ginger root
3 tablespoons coarse salt
2 bay leaves
brine made with 4 oz/125g salt and 2 pints/1.1
   litres water

Wash and scrub 10 of the limes. Cut them downwards, top to bottom, in half, stopping ¼ inch/5 mm from the bottom. Remove any obvious pips. Seed the chillis, cut into thin rounds. Peel and cut the ginger into thin matchsticks. Sprinkle the cut surfaces of the limes with salt and pack them into the jar. Each time a layer has been completed, sprinkle with chillis, ginger and crumbled bay leaf.

Make the brine by boiling a little of the water with the salt to dissolve then mix with the rest of the water. Set aside to cool.

Squeeze the remaining limes one at a time. Add its juice to the pickle. Pour in an equivalent amount of brine. Continue to alternate juice and brine until the fruit is covered, finishing with brine to top up if necessary. Throw away any unwanted brine.

Sterilize a large pebble or stone and place it directly on the limes to keep them submerged in the brine. Cover the jar and leave for at least 10 days.

To serve, take out the limes and cut into slices.

PUNJABI CAULIFLOWER
Serves Four
Cauliflower is especially suited to chilli and hot flavours, as indeed are broccoli and other brassica. Serve it with a pilau and some lentils for a vegetarian meal.
1 cauliflower
1 onion
2 oz/50g butter
2 teaspoons grated fresh ginger root
½ dried red chilli, chopped
1 teaspoon turmeric
½ teaspoon ground cumin

½ teaspoon ground coriander
4 tablespoons chopped fresh coriander
salt
juice of ½ lemon

Trim the cauliflower and break it into florets. Steam it for 3 minutes over boiling water. Reserve.

Peel and chop the onion. Heat the butter in a saucepan and fry the onion for 4 minutes or until transparent. Add the ginger, chilli, turmeric, cumin and ground coriander. Fry for 1 minute. Add the cauliflower, fresh coriander and some salt. Fry for 3 minutes, stirring, in the uncovered pan. Add the lemon juice and 3 tablespoons water. Cover the pan and simmer over a low heat for about 20 minutes, until the cauliflower is tender. Stir occasionally.

FRIED AUBERGINE WITH A GREEN CORIANDER SAUCE
Serves Four
A simplified version of an Indian side dish that answers some of the requirements of a Capricorn recipe. It can be eaten cool as a pungent salad to accompany a plainer meat dish.
1 aubergine
salt
olive oil
black pepper
2 bunches fresh coriander
1 green chilli
10 oz/275g natural yoghurt
juice of ½ lemon
½ teaspoon ground cumin

Cut the aubergine in ¼ inch/5 mm slices, sprinkle with salt and drain in a colander covered by a weighted plate for 30 minutes. Rinse and pat dry.

Pour olive oil into a frying pan to a depth of ½ inch/1 cm. Fry the aubergine slices in the hot oil until golden brown, turning once. Do not try to fry more than one layer at a time. Drain on kitchen paper and season with salt and black pepper.

Strip, wash and dry the coriander, seed the chilli.

Chop the coriander and chilli very fine indeed. Mix with the yoghurt, lemon juice and cumin. Season with salt. Arrange the aubergine on a dish in overlapping rows with some of the sauce on the bottom of each row before placing the next, like roof tiles.

BALKAN POACHED APPLES
Serves Four
2 oz/50g sultanas
8 tablespoons plum brandy or rum
4 large eating apples
8 oz/225g granulated sugar
juice and grated rind of ½ lemon
4 fl oz/120ml whipping cream
1 tablespoon caster sugar

Macerate the sultanas in the spirit for 30 minutes. Peel and core the apples.

In a saucepan, dissolve the sugar in 6 tablespoons of water over gentle heat. Add the lemon juice and rind. Strain the spirit off the sultanas into the syrup. Reserve the sultanas. Put in the apples upright, cover, and cook very gently for about 15 minutes or until just tender but still whole. Take the apples out with a slotted spoon and put onto a dish.

Raise the heat and reduce the syrup by boiling for 5 minutes. Pour over the apples. Leave to cool.

Chill the cream as much as possible, add the sugar and whip until stiff. Fold in the sultanas. Put spoonfuls of the cream into the core cavities of the apples.

ALMOND AND CARDAMOM PUDDING
Serves Four
In contrast to all these sour dishes, here is an aromatic and sweet dish made on a base of ground rice.
1 lb/450g ground rice
4 tablespoons sugar
½ pint/300ml water
½ pint/300ml milk
2 oz/50g blanched almonds, chopped

½ teaspoon ground cardamom seeds
¼ teaspoon pounded saffron threads
1 oz/25g shelled pistachio nuts, blanched and skinned
cream for serving

Mix the ground rice and sugar with half of the water. Put the milk and the remaining water in an uncovered pan to boil. As the liquids come to the boil, whisk in the mixed ground rice and sugar. Turn the heat down and simmer for 2 minutes, stirring all the while. Add the almonds, cardamom and saffron. Cook for a further 5 to 10 minutes over a low heat, stirring to prevent burning.

Spoon the sweet into individual dishes — it should be fairly thick — and decorate with the pistachio nuts. Serve cool with cream.

WEST INDIAN FRUIT SALAD
Serves Four
Another simple dish to recall sunshine on winter days in the north, using citrus fruit that have their origins in the West Indies — grapefruit and ortanique (but you will probably find sweet oranges will have to be substituted).
3 pink grapefruits
4 ortaniques (or 3 good sweet oranges)
5 fl oz/150ml clear honey
1 tablespoon white rum
¼ teaspoon grated nutmeg
caster sugar to taste

Grate the zests of 1 grapefruit and 1 ortanique. Put them in a pan with cold water and boil for 2 minutes. Drain and refresh under cold water. Boil again in fresh water for another 2 minutes. Repeat once more, then drain, refresh and reserve.

Peel the fruit, ridding them of all pith. Cut them into sections, discarding all skin, pips and strings, over a bowl to catch the juices. Arrange the sections on plates as spokes of a wheel.

Whisk the honey into the bowl of juices. Add the blanched zest, rum and nutmeg. Sprinkle the sections with caster sugar to taste and pour over the sauce. Serve chilled.

AQUARIUS

SUN IN AQUARIUS
21 JANUARY - 18 FEBRUARY
RULED BY SATURN

AQUARIUS is a sign of paradoxes, at the same time both deeply conservative and intensely revolutionary, a combination which accounts for its famous eccentricity. Aquarians are individualists and prize their independence above all else. The Arabs noted that they 'like wealth', but were 'anxious about world affairs'. It was also noted that Aquarius is the sign of the gourmet. This is a hot, moist, masculine air sign.

AQUARIUS ENVIRONMENT

Aquarius rules bars, inns, pubs, taverns, vineyards, fish farms and water mills. The sign is associated with running water, so ideal Aquarian places include riverside restaurants and seaside cafés. Many Aquarians enjoy a high-tech environment with luminescent colours and weird lighting effects. Others are more traditional, but even so they like to be unusual, to stand out from the crowd.

AQUARIUS FOODS

The true Aquarian is an experimenter and innovator willing to try any new dish, however modern or exotic, however strange the combination of ingredients. Some revive ancient recipes, others are happier with the latest developments. In the 1960s many Aquarians happily accepted additives which were considered a great step forward in the preservation and presentation of food. In the 1980s many were at the forefront of the wholefood movement. Paradoxically, they are as likely to be strict advocates of macrobiotics as they are to argue the virtues of irradiation in the preservation of food. Aquarius rules aquatic birds such as geese and ducks, salt, which is connected to this sign in homeopathic medicine, and cumin. Other foods associated with this sign are those ruled by Saturn.

A GREEN SOUP

Serves Four

This is based on a Russian recipe, for a light summer soup, made to go further by the addition of a poached egg. If sorrel, which gives a needed acidity, is not available, you can add lemon juice at the end of cooking. Best served with Melba toast and butter.

1 onion
2 carrots
2 sticks celery
1½ pints/900ml ham stock (make sure it is not too salty) or beef stock
1 lb/450g spinach and sorrel
1 tablespoon chopped dill
salt and pepper
4 eggs
5 fl oz/150ml sour cream

Prepare and chop the onion, carrots and celery very finely. Put them with the cold stock in a casserole and boil, uncovered, for 15 minutes. Wash the spinach and sorrel and strip away the larger ribs. Put them in a collander and pour boiling water over them. Chop them fine. Add to the soup and cook at a simmer for another 10 minutes. Add the dill, taste for salt and pepper. Take the casserole off the heat, cover, and put it in a warm oven, 225°F/110°C/Gas Mark ¼, for 20 minutes.

Poach the eggs. Bring the soup up to serving temperature. Pour the soup into a tureen and swirl in the sour cream. Put an egg in each diner's bowl and serve the soup onto it.

FRESHWATER CRAYFISH WITH A LEMON SAUCE

Serves Four

The finest delicacy of Swedish waters is the freshwater crayfish. A great thing is made of them in late summer when the season for catching them is opened — even special crayfish parties by lake and stream. Fresh live crayfish (they must be live) are only available at the very best of fishmongers, so this recipe may have to be adapted for prawns or live Dublin Bay prawns. The sauce is very good. Serve the crayfish with chopped dill, coarse sea salt and rye bread with butter. Remember to have finger bowls and extra napkins on the table.

1 lb/450g crayfish or prawns, in their shell
salt
small *bouquet* of thyme and fennel
4 fl oz/120ml double cream
4 fl oz/120ml stock (see recipe)
grated rind and juice of 1 lemon
4 oz/125g unsalted butter, cut in 8 pieces
salt and pepper
fresh dill for decoration

If your shellfish are live, boil 4 pints/2.3 litres water and 2 teaspoons salt (for freshwater crayfish), treble the salt for saltwater shellfish. Put the shellfish in with the herbs, bring rapidly back to the boil. Boil briskly, uncovered, for about 8 minutes. (Small prawns will need much less time.) Refresh in cold water.

Take the tail shells off and put them in a blender with 4 fluid ounces/120ml boiling water. Blend and strain the stock. Put the double cream and stock in a saucepan and boil for 3 minutes. Add the grated rind and juice of the lemon. Take the pan off the heat and whisk in the butter piece by piece to obtain a smooth sauce. Season with salt and pepper. Keep warm in a bowl set over a pan of hot water.

Serve the crayfish arranged on each plate, with some dill for decoration. Put the tepid lemon sauce in a bowl in the centre of the table with the other condiments.

PRAWN BALLS WITH A TAMARIND SAUCE

Serves Four

This is based on a recipe from the Arabian Gulf using the shellfish favoured by Saturn once more. The sourness imparted by the tamarind is also in tune with the sign and its planet. Tamarind can be bought dried from Oriental food stores, it needs to be treated as described below. Offer some flat Arab bread to mop up the juices.

8 oz/225g frozen prawns, defrosted
1 handful fresh coriander

a good pinch turmeric

2 oz/50g ground rice

½ teaspoon salt

2 shallots

1 oz/25g butter

grated rind of ½ lemon

6 peppercorns, 10 coriander seeds, seeds from 2
    cardamom pods and 2 cloves, ground together

For the sauce

1 piece of dried tamarind 1 inch/2.5cm square

1 small onion

1 tomato

1 oz/25g butter

6 peppercorns, 10 coriander seeds, seeds from 2
    cardamom pods and 2 cloves, ground together

½ dried chilli

salt

1 teaspoon sugar

First make the sauce. Soak the tamarind in 6
fluid ounces/175ml boiling water for 1 hour. Strain
and sieve, retaining the liquid.

Peel and chop the onion; skin, seed and chop
the tomato. Heat the butter in a saucepan and fry
the onion for 5 minutes. Add the tomato, spices
and chilli and fry for 4 minutes. Add the tamarind
water and 6 fluid ounces/175ml cold water. Season
with a pinch of salt and the sugar. Simmer for 15
minutes.

Meanwhile, drain the prawns and pat dry. Blend
to a paste with the fresh coriander, turmeric,
ground rice and salt in a food processor. Peel and
chop the shallots.

Heat the butter in a frying pan and fry the
shallots for 5 minutes, add the lemon rind and
spices and continue cooking 2 minutes. Mix with
the prawn paste. With wet hands, roll into 16 small
balls.

Put the prawn balls in the sauce and poach,
covered, for about 30 minutes.

WELSH SALT DUCK
Serves Four

This Welsh recipe uses salt to produce a
wonderfully delicate duck such as you have never

tasted before (and tender, too, for it tames the
toughest old bird). It can be eaten hot or cold. In
Wales, a dish of laver (the edible seaweed that is
a speciality there) might well come with it, but a
simple orange or watercress salad and some baked
potatoes with butter are good as well.

1 oven-ready duck, without giblets

4-6 oz/125-175g salt

bay leaf

1 stick celery

watercress for serving

Rub the bird with salt all over. Place in the cool
for three days, rubbing salt in and turning the bird
every morning and night.

Wash off the excess salt. Put the duck in a large
casserole with the bay leaf and celery. Cover with
cold water and cook uncovered in a cool oven at
300°F/150°C/Gas Mark 2 for 2 hours, until
tender. Remove the duck and leave to rest or to
cool completely. Serve on a dish with watercress.
It should carve a light pink.

DUCK BRAISED WITH RED CABBAGE
Serves Four

This is a Polish dish. Serve with buttery mashed
potatoes.

It is possible to prepare and cook the cabbage
the previous day, keeping it overnight in the
refrigerator.

1 small red cabbage

2 onions

2 cooking apples

6 rashers streaky bacon

2 tablespoons brown sugar

2 tablespoons ruby port

2 tablespoons red wine vinegar

bouquet of thyme, parsley stalks and marjoram

salt and black pepper

1 roasting duck, about 3-4 lb/1.4-1.8kg

2 tablespoons vegetable oil

Remove the ragged outer leaves of the cabbage.
Quarter, core and slice the cabbage. Then rinse
and drain. Peel and slice the onions; peel, core and
slice the apples; cut the bacon into strips. Mix all

these with the sugar, port and vinegar in a large, heavy casserole. Add the bouquet of herbs and seasoning. Bring to the boil on top of the stove then cover tightly and cook for 2 to 3 hours in a cool oven, 225°F/110°C/Gas Mark ¼.

Rub the duck all over with salt and leave for 30 minutes. Heat the oil in a heavy pan and brown the duck well, on all sides.

Bring the red cabbage back to the boil and place the duck on top. Cover the casserole and replace in the cool oven. Continue to cook for approximately 1½ hours, until the duck is tender. If you have no casserole large enough to hold a whole duck, you can quarter it before frying. It may take less time to cook.

Serve on a large oval platter, the duck surrounded by the red cabbage.

SPICED SPINACH AND PRUNES
Serves Four
Spinach is one of the favoured vegetables of Saturn.
18 jumbo prunes
1 sweet red onion
1½ lb/700g spinach
3 oz/75g butter
1 teaspoon ground cinnamon
¼ teaspoon ground nutmeg
juice of ½ lemon
salt and black pepper
4 eggs
paprika

Soak the prunes overnight in cold water. Cook them for 15 minutes in water. Stone them and cut them in quarters. Put aside. Peel and chop the onion; thoroughly wash and strip the spinach.

In a casserole or large saucepan, fry the onion in 1½ ounces/40g of the butter until transparent for 5 minutes. Add the spices and fry for a minute longer. Add the spinach together with the lemon juice, prunes and seasoning. Cover the pan and cook for about 10 minutes over medium heat.

Butter 4 cocotte dishes and divide the spinach

between them. Make hollows in the centre and break an egg in each. Melt the remaining butter and spoon it over the top. Sprinkle with paprika. Bake for about 4 to 6 minutes (depending on whether you like your eggs thoroughly cooked or not — ideally they should be runny, the whites barely set) in a preheated oven at 375°F/190°C/Gas Mark 5.

JANSSON'S TEMPTATION
Serve Four to Six
A Swedish way with potatoes — said to have tempted one Jansson, a divine who had denied himself all pleasures. Perhaps he too was an Aquarius, and these potatoes the only way to break his obstinate mould.
2 lb/900g potatoes
3 large onions
oil for greasing the dish
2 cans anchovies, 1¾ oz/45g each
pepper
10 fl oz/300ml whipping cream

Peel the potatoes and slice them into matchsticks. Do not rinse. Peel and slice the onions. Mix the potatoes and onions together. Grease a gratin dish and put in two layers of the potato mixture, topped in each instance by a crisscross of anchovies and a grinding of pepper. Pour in half the cream and pour the oil from the anchovy cans over the top.

Bake in a preheated oven at 425°F/220°C/Gas Mark 7 for 20 minutes. Add the remainder of the cream and turn the oven down to 300°F/150°C/Gas Mark 2. Continue baking for 40 minutes or until the potatoes give no resistance when poked through with a knife and the top is a golden brown. Finish under the grill if the crust is too pale. Serve hot.

TOMATO SALAD
Serves Four
The taste of fresh coriander (the most used green herb in world cooking) strikes as having some affinity with Aquarian characteristics. To the

Western palate it has the element of surprise that parsley rarely possesses. This makes a simple tomato salad, but will make your guests rethink the meaning of the description!

6 tomatoes
3 tablespoons chopped fresh coriander
1 small green chilli
1 tablespoon lemon juice
4 tablespoons olive oil
salt

Peel the tomatoes and slice them. Arrange them overlapping on a flat dish. Sprinkle the coriander over the top. Split and seed the chilli and chop it very finely. Mix it with the lemon juice and whisk in the olive oil. Season with salt. Dribble the dressing all over the salad. Leave at room temperature for at least 30 minutes before serving.

STUFFED CABBAGE ROLLS
Serves Four

Stuffed cabbage was introduced to Sweden by the Turkish creditors of a Swedish king at the beginning of the 18th century; they camped on his palace doorstep until he paid up. These cabbage

Northern Fruit Jelly

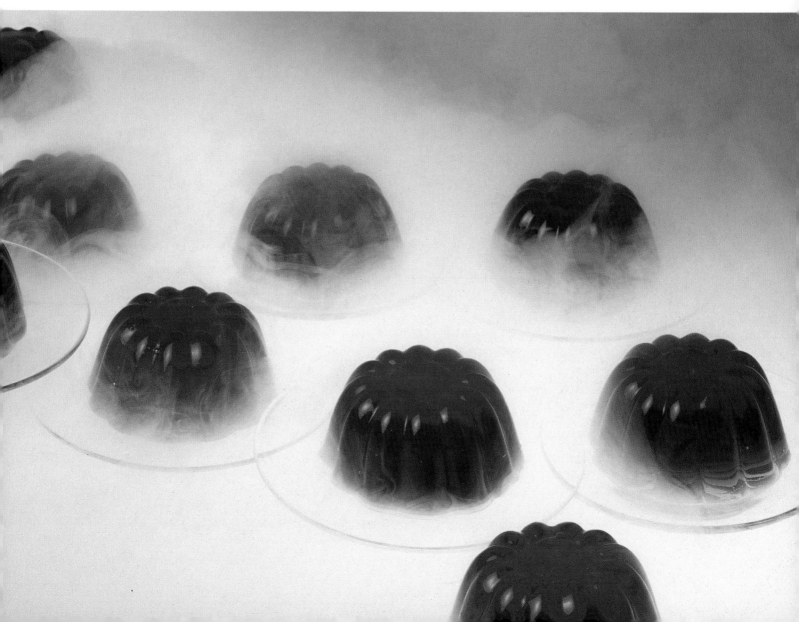

rolls have a resemblance, therefore, to the Greek *dolmades*, or stuffed vine leaves. They are customarily eaten with plain boiled potatoes. You may also care to serve the rest of the cabbage from which you have taken the wrappers cooked in some contrasting, yet simple, fashion.

16 large outer leaves of a Savoy cabbage
salt
3 oz/75g rice
1 onion
8 oz/225g minced beef
6 oz/175g minced pork
1 egg
black pepper
milk
2 oz/50g butter
1 oz/25g brown sugar
10 fl oz/300ml water
5 fl oz/150ml double cream
1 teaspoon paprika

Wash the cabbage leaves and plunge them into boiling salted water for about 2 minutes until pliable. Refresh in cold water and drain.

Cook the rice in salted water for about 15 minutes until tender. Refresh in cold water, drain and put in a bowl. Peel and chop the onion finely and add to the rice with the meats, egg and some salt and pepper. Mix well adding a little milk to make the mixture soft and pliable. Wet your hands if the mixture sticks to them.

Cut out the central rib from each cabbage leaf and lay it flat on the work surface. Shape the stuffing into fingers and place in the centre of each leaf. Fold in the sides then roll the leaves into sausages. Fasten the flaps with cocktail sticks.

Melt the butter in a large frying pan and brown the rolls on all sides over high heat. Arrange them close packed in one layer in a casserole. Sprinkle with the brown sugar. Return the frying pan to the heat. Pour in the water and bring to the boil, stirring and scraping. Pour into the casserole to just cover the cabbage rolls adding more water if necessary. Cover the casserole and simmer over very low heat for 20 to 30 minutes until tender.

To make the gravy, transfer the rolls to a serving dish, reduce the liquor to less than a cupful by boiling hard. Add the cream, seasoning and paprika. Pour over the cabbage rolls and serve.

NORTHERN FRUIT JELLY
Serves Four
Scandinavia, northern Germany, the Baltic region in general, sport a wealth of wild berries delicious in their fruity astringency. Some, like the difficult to obtain lingonberry, are unique to Scandinavia and prized there as a delicacy. Others, like raspberries, have gone on to be tamed, captured for the garden, where domestic varieties are much sweeter and more luscious. But the wild berry often retains an indefinable edge in flavour, perhaps no more than an intimation of nature's generosity. For Aquarians, of course, the greater acidity of the wild, or near wild, fruit is highly fitting. The method for extracting the juice is slow and aims at conserving as far as possible its original flavour.

8-12 oz/225-350g each of bilberries, cranberries, raspberries and strawberries
1 oz/25g powdered gelatine
12 fl oz/350ml near boiling water
cream
sweet biscuits
icing sugar
lemon juice

Put each fruit in a pottery jar, covered with a fitting lid. Place the jars in a pan of simmering water, almost up to the neck. As they gently cook, they will express juice. Periodically pour the juice off, then return the jars to the pan to continue the process which may take up to 1 hour. You will have enough when you have 10 fluid ounces/300ml from each fruit.

In each of 4 bowls, dissolve ¼ oz/7g gelatine in 3 fluid ounces/75ml of the very hot water. Add a little of each fruit juice to its gelatine, stirring until completely dissolved, then stir in the rest. Taste each in turn, adding sufficient icing sugar and, if necessary (for instance with the bilberries), lemon juice. Bear in mind that they will taste less sweet when chilled.

Leave them to cool, but not in the refrigerator. Rinse a jelly mould with cold water. Put in the first of the jellies, strawberry. Leave to set in the refrigerator. Then add the next layer, raspberry. When that has set, the third layer, cranberry, can be poured in, and so on to the last, bilberry. Cover the mould with clingfilm and leave in the refrigerator until set.

To turn out, hold the mould in a bowl of hot water for as short a time as possible (5 to 10 seconds if the mould is metal, longer for china) then unmould onto a dish. Serve with pouring cream and sweet biscuits.

LOGANBERRY KISSEL
Serves Four

The same taste for red fruits and wild fruits touched on by Northern Fruit Jelly (*see* previous page) is seen in some of the cooking of the USSR. Kissel, although perhaps German in origin, is a naturalized Russian dish and a useful standby, especially if your fruit is overripe, more refreshing than a cream or custard fool. In Russia, some very tart wild fruits — cherries, barberries and so on — are used. Arrowroot is the suggested thickening agent, but you can use potato flour, and a kissel can be made with cornflour too.

6 oz/175g loganberries (but any red or soft fruit will do)
4 fl oz/120ml red wine
10 fl oz/300ml water
4 oz/125g caster sugar
2 tablespoons arrowroot
juice of ½ orange
4 slices white bread
butter
caster sugar mixed with ground cinnamon
cream for serving

Pick over the fruit, removing stalks and leaves, and purée in a blender. Strain the juice and reserve. Put the pulp into a saucepan with the wine and water. Bring to the boil and cook uncovered for 4 minutes. Strain and return the liquid to the pan. Add the sugar to the hot liquid and stir to dissolve. Mix the arrowroot in the orange juice. Stir it into the syrup. Bring to the boil and cook for 1 minute. Add in the reserved fruit juice, pour into glasses and leave to cool.

Toast the bread on one side only. Butter the other side. Sprinkle generously with the sugar and cinnamon mixture. Put back under a low heat and toast to a golden brown. Cut into quarters and serve hot with the kissel along with some cream.

SALZBURG DUMPLINGS
Serves Four

These 'dumplings' are ethereal puffs of sweet egg — a definitive answer to the sweet omelette, or a simple soufflé. The ascetic side of Saturn, loving small portions, is here met by the fact that this will only just feed four.

4 egg yolks
1 tablespoon kirsch
6 egg whites
pinch of salt
3 oz/75g vanilla sugar
2 tablespoons flour
1 oz/25g butter
3 fl oz/85ml single cream
icing sugar for dredging

Beat the yolks together with the kirsch until light and creamy. Whisk the whites with the salt until really stiff. Add 2 ounces/50g of the sugar by degrees and continue whisking. Success relies on a light and stiff egg white. Fold the yolks into the whites, ensuring complete absorption but without beating. Sift the flour over the top and fold that in. Melt the butter in a pan. Add the cream and the rest of the sugar. Stir to dissolve as it heats to near boiling.

Have a large oval gratin dish already warmed. Pour in the cream mixture, covering the bottom entirely. Spoon in the soufflé mixture in three piles — they will spread to form one. Bake in a preheated hot oven, 425°F/220°C/Gas Mark 7 for about 7 minutes. Dredge with icing sugar before serving.

PISCES

SUN IN PISCES 19 FEBRUARY - 20 MARCH
RULED BY JUPITER

PISCES is a cold, moist, mutable, feminine water sign. It is the most sensitive, compassionate and sympathetic of all the signs, although Pisceans often develop a cold veneer or put on an act to conceal their deep emotions. The happiest are those painters, musicians and writers who have a creative means to express their imaginations. Some find an outlet in the culinary arts, and Piscean chefs produce some of the most exotic and inventive dishes.

PISCES ENVIRONMENTS

As a water sign Pisces rules all places by water and all damp or wet environments. Typical Pisceans like to eat out where there is a view of water, or where water is essential to the environment: in converted water mills or pump houses, on houseboats, near harbours or at the end of piers. They tend to be fussy about their surroundings. When out they appreciate peace and quiet, soft lighting, civilized music, considerate service and a romantic atmosphere. They are far from bland and are fond of anything unusual or exotic which stimulates their artistic imaginations. At home their decorative ambitions are often sabotaged by their untidy habits, and the Piscean dining room is often a place of homely chaos.

PISCES FOODS

Pisces is a sensitive sign and Pisceans often develop aversions to particular foods. They are prone to food fads and tend to become vegetarians and followers of gimicky diets. When they swing to the other extreme, they become gluttons, gourmands rather than gourmets, but such a life style soon catches up with them. Pisces rules sea birds and fish, including trout, salmon and tuna. It also rules sugar, most fruits and artichokes, cabbage, gourds and turnips. It is associated with alcohol, as well as drinks in general, although these are, strictly speaking, ruled by Aquarius. Fish cooked in a wine sauce is ideally Piscean.

GRILLED SCALLOPS WITH SZECHWAN PEPPER
Serves Four

Pisces is the sign of the fish and hence protector of fishermen, sea ports and fishing communities everywhere. Understandably, many of the recipes in this chapter are fish based and some cuisines are more dependent on that ingredient than others — not least Japan, largely meat free but with wonderful raw and cooked fish dishes. The love of Jupiter for pure foods is well matched by Japanese sashimi and, here, this dish of briefly cooked scallops.

8 large scallops
2 tablespoons soy sauce
3 tablespoons *sake*—Japanese rice wine
Szechwan or Japanese pepper, available from
  Chinese food stores

For the sauce
½ sweet onion
vegetable oil
1 tablespoon chopped parsley
1 teaspoon chopped fresh coriander
3 fl oz/85ml *sake*
the roes of the scallops
salt

Separate the roes and muscles of the scallops. Wash the muscles and pat dry. Cut in half horizontally. Mix the soy and *sake* in a bowl and marinate the scallops for 5 minutes.

Meanwhile, make the sauce. Chop the onion finely. Cook it in oil on a gentle heat, without colouring, until soft. Add the chopped parsley, coriander and the *sake*. Boil to reduce slightly. Add the roes and simmer for 2 minutes. Press through a fine sieve or blend to a purée. Add seasoning to taste.

Lift out the scallops and thread onto 4 small wooden skewers. Cook under a hot grill for about 4 minutes. Turn frequently, brushing them with the marinade each time.

For each person: put a spoonful of sauce on a plate, place 4 scallop slices on top, sprinkle with Szechwan pepper and serve.

COD WITH A SHRIMP SAUCE
Serves Four

Fish with fish — an English standard once served everywhere — is an ideal Piscean combination.

2 fl oz/50ml wine vinegar
½ horseradish root, washed
2 oz/50g salt
4 very fresh cod steaks, each about 6 oz/175g
  minimum

For the sauce
6 oz/175g fresh cooked shrimps
2 shallots
1 oz/25g butter
½ pint/300ml water
1 anchovy fillet
5 fl oz/150ml double cream
½ teaspoon tomato purée
black pepper
squeeze of lemon

First make the sauce. Shell the shrimps and set aside. Reserve the shells and heads. Peel and chop the shallots. Melt the butter in a saucepan. Add the shallots and cook gently until soft. Add the water, the anchovy fillet and the shells and heads of the shrimps. Simmer, covered, for 20 minutes. Strain the liquid and return to the heat. Boil to reduce by two-thirds. Stir in the cream and tomato purée and simmer until the sauce is smooth and thick. Season with pepper and lemon juice and keep hot.

Meanwhile, in a pan large enough to hold the cod in one layer, put the vinegar, horseradish, salt and the fish with enough cold water to cover. Bring to the boil over high heat. Turn off the heat as it comes to the boil and cover the pan. Remove the cod when it is tender in about 5 minutes.

Add the shrimps to the sauce at the last moment so as not to toughen them. Serve the fish on hot plates, the sauce separately.

MACKEREL WITH GOOSEBERRY SAUCE
Serves Four

In Normandy in northern France the gooseberry is called 'mackerel currant'. Though figuring rarely in French recipes, it is accepted as a natural accompaniment to the mackerel. It is also a fruit of Jupiter, the ruler of Pisces. Mackerel must be eaten very fresh. Herring might be better in districts away from sea ports, even if the taste of the dish changes.

4 mackerel, each about 8 oz/225g
½ bottle dry white wine
1 tablespoon wine vinegar
1 small onion
salt

For the butter sauce
3 oz/75g butter
2 tablespoons chopped fennel
1 tablespoon chopped parsley
salt
cayenne pepper
lemon juice

For the gooseberry sauce
6 oz/175g gooseberries
1 oz/25g butter
1 tablespoon sugar
1 tablespoon chopped chives
3 tablespoons whipping cream
salt and black pepper
2 egg yolks

To make the butter sauce, melt the butter and mix in the herbs, salt, cayenne pepper and a squeeze of lemon juice. Let it steep then adjust the seasoning just before serving.

To make the gooseberry sauce, put the gooseberries in a pan with the butter and sugar. Cook, covered, over gentle heat for about 5 minutes or until reduced to a purée. Add the chives and cook for another 2 minutes. Put the gooseberries through the fine plate of food mill into a bowl. Add the cream, seasoning and egg yolks. Set the bowl in a pan of hot water over low heat and cook gently until the sauce has thickened slightly. On no account should it boil or the eggs will scramble.

Meanwhile, gut the mackerel, leave their heads on. Mix the white wine with an equal amount of water and the vinegar. Peel and slice the onion and add to the liquid. Add salt. Bring to the boil in a wide pan and put in the mackerel. Cover and simmer very gently for about 7 minutes.

Serve the mackerel with the butter sauce spooned over it, and serve the gooseberry sauce separately.

OYSTERS WITH RED BUTTER
Serves Four

Also from Normandy comes this recipe for oysters. It combines the rich food beloved of Jupiter and the natural choice of Pisces to exactitude. The red butter sauce, easy to make and luxurious to eat, goes well with many things, not least crisply grilled fillet steak. It is very much better if the butter is best unsalted French or Dutch. Serve these oysters with waffles, Scotch pancakes or Russian buckwheat pancakes and a small undressed salad of thinly sliced endive with watercress.

16-24 large Pacific oysters
2 oz/50g shallots
4 fl oz/120ml light red wine
6 oz/175g unsalted butter, cut in small pieces
lemon juice
salt and black pepper

Open the oysters and empty the muscle and strained liquor into a small pan and reserve.

Peel and chop the shallots very thinly. Put them in a saucepan with the red wine and boil, uncovered, to reduce the liquid to at the most a tablespoonful. Take the pan off the heat and add the butter piece by piece, beating with a wooden spoon all the time. Return the pan to the heat if necessary but keep the heat low so that the butter comes into a creamy sauce which neither melts into something greasy, nor remains unmelted. When each piece is absorbed, add the next. Season with a squeeze of lemon, salt and black pepper. Pour the sauce into a bowl set over hot water.

Heat the oysters very quickly and briefly. There is no need to 'cook' them as such, merely to make them hot. Divide them between 4 small bowls, adding a spoonful of the liquor to each bowl. Spoon the red butter over them.

TURBOT COOKED IN CIDER, SERVED WITH APPLE

Serves Four

The way in which this turbot is cooked is nearly the national standard in Normandy — a province of orchards and dairies. Instead of turbot, brill, John Dory or any other firm white fish can be used, but the less firm it is, the greater the care must be taken not to overcook it. As a first course, it needs no accompaniment.

1½ pints/900ml dry cider
salt
2 turbot steaks or fillets, each about 10 oz/275g

2 Cox's Orange Pippin apples
2 oz/50g butter
2 tomatoes
1 teaspoon brandy
5 fl oz/150ml chicken stock
7 fl oz/200ml double cream
juice of ¼ lemon
black pepper
parsley sprigs

In a large pan, bring the cider and ½ teaspoon salt to the boil. Turn down the heat and gently lower in the turbot steaks. Cover the pan and cook

Turbot Cooked in Cider, Served with Apple

at no more than a simmer for about 10 minutes or until the flesh comes away from the back bone. When cooked, lift out the turbot and keep warm in a covered dish. Reserve the cooking liquor.

Peel, core and cut the apples in rounds, then halve the rounds. Melt the butter in a small pan and fry the apples for about 5 minutes until just tender without breaking up, keep warm.

Put half the reserved cooking liquor in a pan. Boil, uncovered, to reduce to half a cupful. Roughly chop the tomatoes and add them to the pan, with the brandy and stock. Boil uncovered for 4 minutes. Strain and return the sauce to the heat. Stir in 5 fluid ounces/150ml of the cream and the lemon juice. Cook until the sauce is smooth and slightly thick. Taste and season with salt and pepper. Beat in the remaining double cream just before serving.

Remove the skin and bone from the turbot. Pour the sauce onto 4 plates. Arrange the fish over the sauce. Lay the apple slices and parsley sprigs on top of the fish and serve.

PORTUGUESE LOBSTER
Serves Four

In Portugal you can eat matchlessly fresh fish and shellfish – spider crabs, lobsters, crayfish, large prawns and scallops. Often they are prepared with tomato, herbs and onion. Serve this dish with boiled potatoes and lots of mange tout peas with butter.

4 onions
4 large tomatoes
4 cloves garlic
1 fl oz/25ml olive oil
6 fl oz/175ml port wine
2 sprigs thyme
2 sprigs tarragon
salt and pepper
sugar
2 live lobsters, each about 1½ lbs/700g

Peel and slice the onions; skin, seed and chop the tomatoes; peel and halve the garlic. Heat the oil in a casserole and cook the onions over low

heat for 25 minutes. Add the tomatoes, garlic, port wine, herbs and seasoning. Bring to the boil, cover tightly and stew in a cool preheated oven, 225°F/110°C/Gas Mark ¼, for at least 1 hour. Return the casserole to the top of the stove. Discard the herbs then boil briskly to reduce any surplus liquid. Taste for seasoning, adding a little sugar if the tomatoes require it.

Bring a large pan of water to the boil. Put in the lobsters and bring back to the boil as quickly as possible. Boil for 30 seconds, then remove the lobsters; this kills them and firms the flesh slightly to make it easier to extract. Split the lobsters in half lengthwise. Remove and discard the sac and the intestinal duct. Remove the flesh from body, head and legs. Cut the body into large collops. Put the lobster meat on top of the tomato and onion mixture, also adding the cream from the head. Cover the casserole again and return to the cool oven for at least 15, if not 20 minutes, until the lobster is cooked.

TABBOULEH or COUSCOUS SALAD
Serves Four

The cracked wheat, mint and tomato salad called Tabbouleh is a Lebanese dish in origin. The traders of that country, having spread their roots to the coastal zones of East, West and North Africa, have taken their favourite foods with them. The African version uses couscous, leaf coriander and cucumber.

7 oz/200g couscous
10-20 fl oz/300-600ml cold water
4 tablespoons lemon juice
  plus the juice of 1 lemon
8 tablespoons olive oil
salt and black pepper
2 bunches parsley
25 mint leaves
1 tablespoon chopped fresh coriander
12 spring onions
3 tomatoes
½ cucumber
½ cos lettuce

In a bowl, soak the couscous in the water for 30 minutes. Squeeze the couscous and pour off the surplus water. Add the 4 tablespoons lemon juice, oil, salt and black pepper. Leave for another 10 to 15 minutes.

Wash and chop the parsley and mint coarsely. Add them and the coriander to the couscous. Slice the white parts of the spring onions finely; skin, seed and chop the tomatoes, saving any juice that runs off; seed and dice the cucumber. Add all to the couscous. Leave the couscous in the cool for at least 2 hours for the flavours to mix.

Serve in a bowl surrounded with cos lettuce. Mix the remaining lemon juice and a little salt in a bowl and hand it round as a dressing.

CARROTS WITH A CIDER SAUCE
Serves Four
The alcoholic content of this Norman way with carrots makes it ideally suited to Pisces.
1 onion
2 oz/50g butter
½ oz/15g flour
8 fl oz/250ml dry cider
salt and pepper
nutmeg
lemon juice
1 lb/450g carrots
1 tablespoon double cream

Peel and chop the onion. Heat half the butter in a saucepan and fry the onion for about 5 minutes or until transparent. Add the flour and meld with the butter. Add the cider gradually, stirring the while. Cook to a smooth sauce over low heat for 8 minutes. Cut the remaining butter into pieces and beat into the sauce. Season with salt, pepper and nutmeg. Add a squeeze of lemon if it lacks piquancy.

Scrub or peel and trim the carrots. Cut them into matchsticks. Put them in boiling salted water for between 3 and 4 minutes, until just cooked but still giving some resistance. Drain and add them to the sauce. Stir in the double cream just before serving.

CAMEMBERT TOAST
Serves Four
A savoury made with the Norman cheese, Camembert. Serve toast, with watercress salad.
4 slices bread
4 oz/125g unripe Camembert
3 fl oz/85ml double cream
2 egg yolks
1 teaspoon Dijon mustard
salt and pepper
nutmeg

Trim the bread. Toast on both sides. Take the rind off the cheese. Melt with the other ingredients in a saucepan. Cook gently, stirring, for 3 minutes, but do not let it boil. Spread on the toast and finish under the grill. Cut the toast into fingers.

SWEET CUSTARD WITH ANIS
Serves Four
Jupiter likes rich foods, greasy foods and sweet foods. Sugar cane is normally reckoned part of the planet's palette. So, too, is aniseed. This very sweet custard from Portugal is flavoured with an *anis*-based liqueur. The Portuguese go in for extremely sweet desserts, a little, therefore, may go further than you expect.
6 oz/175g sugar
5 fl oz/150ml milk
5 fl oz/150ml double cream
5 egg yolks
2 tablespoons any *anis* liqueur

Melt the sugar with 2 tablespoons water and cook to a golden brown syrup. Mix the milk and cream and heat to boiling. Add the syrup and beat together. Beat the egg yolks well and whisk into the milk and syrup mixture, and add the liqueur. Pour into 8 individual moulds. Stand the moulds in a roasting pan. Pour in enough hot water to come two-thirds up the sides of the moulds. Cover with greaseproof paper and bake in a preheated oven at 325°F/160°C/Gas Mark 3 for about 30 minutes or until they are set and a skewer inserted into the centre of the custards comes out clean. Chill, unmould and serve.

STRAWBERRIES AND ORANGES IN ASTI SPUMANTE

Serves Four

The sign's ruling planet Jupiter has strawberries and oranges within its realm — fortunate indeed. Ally this with the Piscean affection for alcohol and you have a simple summer cup with Asti Spumante — a much better wine than its reputation would have us believe, so long as you buy a good one.

3 oranges
12 oz/350g strawberries
2 oz/50g caster sugar
1 bottle Asti Spumante

Peel the oranges, removing all pith. Section them by cutting the flesh away from the inner divisions. Save the flesh and the juice in a bowl. Wipe and hull the strawberries. Cut them in halves or quarters. Mix with the oranges. Add the sugar and leave in the bowl for 15 minutes.

Divide the fruit between 4 really large glasses. At the moment of serving, pour on the Asti Spumante and carry foaming to the table.

PORTUGUESE ORANGE PUDDING

Serves Four

Another very sweet Portuguese custard, according with Jupiter's love of sweet richness.

8 oz/225g sugar
5 eggs
juice and grated rind of 1 orange
butter for greasing
sugar for dusting

Beat the first 3 ingredients together. Butter a mould and sprinkle sugar over the inside — it will stick to the butter. Pour in the mixture and bake at 325°F/160°C/Gas Mark 3 for about 40 minutes or until a knife inserted into the centre comes out clean. Leave to cool then cut into squares.

MEDITERRANEAN SWEETMEATS

Enough for Twelve

A final celebration of Jupiter's sweet tooth and of the cooking skills of the countries bordering the Mediterranean. These need presenting in individual sweetmeat papers and serving with coffee and a glass of iced water.

Fig balls
2 oz/50g dried figs
2 oz/50g toasted blanched almonds
1 oz/25g plain chocolate
grated zest of orange
2 oz/50g sugar plus extra for coating

Break up the first 3 ingredients and grind them fine with a pinch of grated orange zest. Boil the sugar and 1 tablespoon of water until it just starts to turn in colour. Mix everything together and leave it to cool. Roll into 12 little balls and roll to coat with sugar.

Stuffed apricots
2 oz/50g ground almonds
1 oz/25g caster sugar
1 tablespoon rosewater
1 oz/25g pistachio nuts, blanched and skinned
12-16 dried stoned apricots

Mix the almonds, sugar and rosewater. Chop the pistachio nuts fine. Stuff the apricots with the almond mixture and coat their open tops with the pistachio.

Stuffed dates
2 oz/50g plain chocolate
1 fl oz/25ml double cream
½ oz/15g unsalted butter
1 tablespoon brandy
1 oz/25g chestnuts, chopped
16 dates, stoned

Melt the chocolate, cream, butter and brandy in a bowl over hot water. Leave to cool, mix in the chestnuts. Stuff the dates with the mixture.

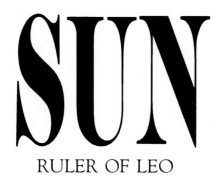

SUN

RULER OF LEO

THE SUN is the most powerful of all the planets. It is active, extrovert, proud, generous, warm hearted and rules the creative force. It has a general rulership over all food and is associated with the acts of eating and drinking.

SUN ENVIRONMENTS
The Sun rules all magnificent buildings, such as palaces and grand theatres. In the home the dining room is ruled by the Sun. Where the Sun dominates, fabrics are rich and colours warm and bright.

SUN COOKING
Spit-roasting, dry roasting or baking are typical solar methods of food preparation.

SUN FOODS
Foods ruled by the Sun are typically dry and tend to be yellow in colour. True solar food boosts the body's vital force, strengthening the heart, improving the eyesight and eliminating poisons and toxins. All aromatic and sweet-and-sour food is associated with the Sun.

SUN MEAT, FISH AND POULTRY
Solar animals tend to be male, for example, rams, bulls and cocks.

SUN VEGETABLES, GRAINS, ETC
Sugar cane, sunflower seeds, and some grains including barley, maize and rice.

SUN FRUITS AND NUTS
Oranges, lemons, cherries, mangoes, pomegranates, bananas and olives are typical solar fruits. The Sun rules all nuts but especially almonds, coconuts and walnuts.

SUN HERBS, SPICES AND FLAVOURINGS, ETC
Sugar, saffron, turmeric, mustard, ginger, rosemary, cinnamon, bay leaves, camomile, lovage, mace, nutmeg, peppermint, vervain, sage and rue.

CRAB CLAWS WITH GINGER

Serves Four

The use of ginger is the justification for including this recipe, for the Sun loves ginger and many aromatic spices. It can be made with a whole crab if that is more convenient. In the manner of Far Eastern crab and lobster dishes, it is quite messy to eat, so be sure to provide finger bowls and napkins.

8 crab claws, ready boiled
3 tablespoons vegetable oil
4 spring onions
1 clove garlic
2 knobs stem ginger preserved in syrup
1 teaspoon curry powder
6 fl oz/175ml port wine
1 teaspoon dark soy sauce
juice of ¼ lemon
1 tablespoon ginger syrup
salt and pepper
watercress

In a large pan fry the crab claws in the oil for 4 minutes, making sure they are thoroughly hot. Lift out the claws, wrap in a cloth and keep warm.

Slice the spring onions; peel and chop the garlic; chop the stem ginger finely. In the same pan, fry the onion and garlic, without burning, for 2 minutes. Add the curry powder and fry for another minute. Stir in the port wine and the chopped ginger. Boil to reduce the liquid by half.

Add the soy sauce, lemon juice and ginger syrup and bring to the boil again. Taste for seasoning.

Crack the crab claws cleanly with the back of a heavy kitchen knife. Add them to the pan and stir round to coat thoroughly with the scant and sticky sauce. Serve with lots of watercress.

YELLOW FLOWER SALAD AND GOAT CHEESE TOAST

Serves Four

The Sun's propensity for the masculine element seems also to have tilted it towards the goat — though the male plays small part in the production of the cheese! So a dry roasted cheese is here combined with the colour of the Sun in the flowers included in the salad. Early in the season there will be primrose, daisy and broom — buds or flowers. Too many broom flowers at one time are not good for you, so do not add more than a dozen. Later in the summer, marigold, nasturtium and daisy will be the ones. You can also use the young leaves of those I have noted. The alliance of walnuts with cheese has always been good and as they, too, are favoured by the Sun, the dish may be thought a solar counterpoint of flavours and colours.

For the cheese
4 slices of rye or wholemeal bread
butter
4 individual *Crottins de Chavignol* or 4 slices of
    goat's cheese *rouleau*, each about 2 oz/50g
black pepper

For the salad
1 sprig lovage
salad leaves, including young lettuce, sorrel,
    spinach, corn salad and chicory *or* 1 small cos
    lettuce and 1 small head of red chicory
yellow flowers, including primrose (and young
    leaves), broom, common daisy, pot (not French)
    marigold petals (and young leaves) or nasturtium
    (and leaves)
1 tablespoon broken walnuts
4 tablespoons olive oil
1 tablespoon walnut oil
1 tablespoon wine vinegar
salt and black pepper

Cut off the crusts, toast the bread on both sides and butter it. Put the cheese on a baking sheet in the oven preheated to 450°F/230°C/Gas Mark 8 for 3 to 5 minutes until melting at the edges. Place each piece of cheese on a slice of toast. Grind black pepper over the top.

Rub the bowl in which you are to mix the salad with the lovage (it tastes and smells very strongly of celery). Put in your choice of salad leaves and flowers. Add the walnuts. To make the dressing whisk the oils into the vinegar, season to taste (goat's cheese is often salty), pour over the salad and toss to mix.

TANDOORISED CHICKEN

Serves Four

To keep to the Sun's specifications, the bird cooked here should be a cockerel. It would be foolish to claim that the recipe is just as performed in the *tandoors* of Pakistan, nonetheless it uses some of their ingredients and techniques and produces a really good spiced roast chicken. A closer approximation may be had if the chicken is spit-roasted over charcoal or jointed and charcoal grilled. The true tandoori colour is red, this one will be nearer the Sun's yellow. Serve with a tomato and onion salad and a dish of spinach.

1 large chicken, at least 3½ lb/1.6kg
3 inch/7.5cm piece fresh ginger root, peeled
4 cloves garlic, peeled
4 tablespoons lemon juice
6 ground cloves
1 tablespoon ground coriander
1 teaspoon turmeric
1 teaspoon ground cumin
½ teaspoon ground cinnamon
½ teaspoon cayenne pepper
1 teaspoon salt
½ teaspoon ground black pepper
5 oz/150g yoghurt

Tandoorised Chicken

6 tablespoons vegetable oil
1 lemon, cut in wedges

Remove the skin from the chicken. Slash the fleshy parts of the carcase with a knife so that the marinade can enter. Blend the ginger, garlic and lemon juice together to a purée. Add the ground spices, seasonings, yoghurt and 3 tablespoons of the oil. Mix well together and rub into the chicken really well. Cover and leave the chicken sitting in the marinade in a large bowl in the refrigerator for 24 hours. Every 8 to 12 hours, repeat the rubbing-in.

Preheat the oven to 400°F/200°C/Gas Mark 6. Put the rest of the oil in a roasting pan. Roast the chicken for about 45 to 60 minutes, basting with the marinade every 10 to 15 minutes. Serve with the lemon wedges.

BEST END OF LAMB AUX HERBES DE PROVENCE
Serves Four

This dish encapsulates a way of cooking the planet loves best, in combination with the aromatic herbs it nourishes on the sun drenched slopes of Provence in southern France. Although an easy dish to present well, it depends on the meat being properly butchered. It has become almost customary to serve a *gratin dauphinois* with the lamb although some turned roasted potatoes would be more fitting here, perhaps flavoured with a touch of garlic and rosemary. Yellow tomatoes, baked with basil and butter, would be reinforcement of the Sun's message.

2 best ends of lamb, each of 8 cutlets
7 tablespoons soft breadcrumbs
2 tablespoons chopped parsley
2 scant teaspoons dried *herbes de Provence*
salt and pepper
2 oz/50g butter, melted
1 tablespoon oil
6 fl oz/175ml water
4 fl oz/120ml red wine
2 oz/50g butter

Have the butcher prepare the lamb in the classic manner. Remove the backbone and associated nerve; trim all flesh, fat and gristle from between the rib bones beyond the nut of meat; chop the rib bones themselves so that only 2 inches/5cm stick out; skin and cut away any superfluous fat over the meat itself, leaving just a thin layer. Save the bones and debris.

Mix the breadcrumbs, herbs, salt and pepper together. Brush the back of the lamb with melted butter and press into the crumb mixture to coat evenly. Put the bones and debris in a roasting pan with the oil, place the best ends on top of them, crumbs uppermost. Roast in a preheated oven at 425°F/220°C/Gas Mark 7 for 20 minutes.

Put the meat to rest on a rack, covered, in a warm place for at least 15 minutes.

Meanwhile, drain the fat from the roasting pan. Put the pan over heat, add the water and stir and scrape vigorously. Reduce by boiling until only 2 tablespoons of liquid are left. Add the wine, boil and reduce by half. Strain the sauce into a clean bowl and whisk in the butter, a little at a time. Taste for seasoning.

Carve the meat, arrange on a serving dish, and serve the sauce separately.

CARROTS AND COURGETTES WITH A MINT SAUCE
Serves Four

Peppermint is a Sun flavour. This way with two vegetables gives a chance for a simple mint cream sauce to show its paces.

2 shallots
1 stick celery
6 fl oz/175ml white wine
4 fl oz/120ml vegetable stock
6 mint leaves
1 tablespoon double cream
salt and pepper
2½ oz/65g butter
4 large carrots
4 large courgettes

Peel and chop the shallots; chop the celery. Put them in a pan with the wine and vegetable stock.

Boil rapidly until there is only 5 tablespoons of liquid remaining. Strain and discard the vegetables; return the liquid to the pan. Cut the mint leaves into ribbons and add to the pan with the cream. Cook for 30 seconds, season with salt and pepper, then whisk in ½ ounce/15g of the butter.

Peel and cut the carrots into extremely fine and long matchsticks. If you have a crinkled blade on a *mandoline* use that. Wipe and treat the courgettes in the same fashion. Cook the carrots in a steamer for about 4 to 6 minutes, depending on the size of the sticks. Cook the courgettes in the remaining butter in a large pan. Fry quite rapidly for 3 minutes, but do not colour. Season with salt and pepper. Lightly mix the carrots and courgettes together with the sauce and serve.

LEMON CURD TART
Serves Four
The simple combination of eggs, sugar and lemon has lately come back into favour in our kitchens, having once been a standard of 18th century cooking. It is the most luxurious way of experiencing the richness of flavour of the lemon, fruit of the Sun.
8 oz/225g sweet shortcrust pastry
3 oz/75g sugar
2 oz/50g unsalted butter
1 whole egg plus 1 yolk
grated rind and juice of 1 small lemon

Roll the pastry out to fit a 10 inch/25cm tart case. Prick the bottom and rest for 20 minutes in the cool. Line the pastry case with aluminium foil, weigh down with dried beans and bake blind in a preheated oven at 400°F/200°C/Gas Mark 6 for about 15 minutes. Uncover the pastry and continue baking for 5 more minutes or until lightly coloured.

Cream the sugar and butter in a bowl set over a pan of simmering water. Add the eggs and lemon. Cook for about 20 minutes or until thickened.

Fill the tart case with this curd, then leave to cool before serving.

CHESTNUT AND CHOCOLATE CAKE
Serves at least Four
This is a rich mould rather than cake, celebrating one of the nuts so favoured by the Sun. Serve it with an ice cold Chantilly cream flavoured with cinnamon.

For the plain chestnut layer
8 oz/225g chestnuts
milk
2 oz/50g vanilla sugar
1 fl oz/25ml water
2 oz/50g unsalted butter

For the chocolate and chestnut layer
2 oz/50g plain chocolate
1 oz/25g vanilla sugar
1 fl oz/25ml water
6 oz/175g unsweetened chestnut purée
1 teaspoon brandy

For the chocolate coating
2 oz/50g plain chocolate
½ teaspoon sugar
1 tablespoon water
½ oz/15g butter

Peel and skin the chestnuts by scoring them and blanching them in boiling water for 1 minute. Put them in a pan, cover with milk and simmer for about 1 hour until extremely soft. Drain and put through a food mill to make a purée.

Combine the sugar and water in a pan and boil for 4 minutes over medium heat. Mix the syrup and the butter into the chestnuts.

To make the chocolate and chestnut layer, melt the chocolate, sugar and water together in a double boiler. Beat into the unsweetened chestnut purée with the brandy.

Line a 1 pound/450g loaf tin with clingfilm. Put in layers of the 2 mixtures, starting and finishing with the plain chestnut. Leave to set in the refrigerator, for at least 1 hour.

For the coating, melt the chocolate with the sugar and water. Beat in the butter. Unmould the cake and spread this mixture over it with a palette knife. Serve in thin slices.

MOON

RULER OF CANCER

THE MOON is a caring, nurturing planet and in psychology is associated with the archetype of the mother. Its character is emotional, soft and sensitive. It is also cold and moist, ruling water and all wet places and conditions.

MOON ENVIRONMENTS
The Moon rules places such as fishing villages, ports, lush countryside, rivers, ponds, pools, springs and lakes. It is also associated with hotels and boarding houses and in the home it rules kitchens.

MOON COOKING
Lunar food is typically cold and moist. It is often uncooked, for example, salads or Japanese raw fish. The food is likely to be marinated and, if cooked, boiling or poaching are appropriate methods.

MOON FOODS
These are generally fresh, succulent and juicy. They have a bland, watery, slightly sweet taste, and grow in watery places. The Moon rules drinks overall and is also associated with dairy products.

MOON MEAT, FISH AND POULTRY
Lunar creatures live on or near water, so all fish, sea birds, and animals are included, especially frogs, snails, geese, ducks, oysters, crabs, lobsters, cockles and eels. Shellfish are ruled jointly by the Moon and Saturn. The Moon also rules beef, chicken, ham and rabbit.

MOON VEGETABLES, GRAINS, ETC.
The Moon rules trailing plants and succulent vegetables with thick juicy leaves. Lunar vegetables include marrow, cucumber, pumpkin and all varieties of squash, onion, lettuce, leeks, mushrooms, chicory, endive, tomato, cabbage, cauliflower, watercress, kale, seaweed and potato. The Arabs also associated the Moon with wheat and barley.

MOON FRUITS AND NUTS
All watery and succulent fruits, especially melons, are Moon fruits. On occasion the Moon also rules unripe fruit. Water chestnuts are also lunar.

MOON HERBS, SPICES AND FLAVOURINGS, ETC.
The Moon rules bland flavours so is not usually associated with herbs and spices. The exceptions are hyssop, rosemary and poppy seeds.

OYSTERS WITH A WATERCRESS CREAM
Serves Four

Oysters and watercress are a lunar combination. Small elaboration is needed to add cucumber and seaweed — a lunar full house. It should be eaten at just above room temperature, no need to be hot.

3 bunches watercress
1 oz/25g butter
3 medium potatoes
1 pint/600ml water
salt and pepper
24 oysters
3 tablespoons double cream
chervil sprigs to decorate

Wash the watercress and rid it of its larger stalks. Reserve one-third and put the rest in a saucepan to cook gently with the butter for 3 minutes.

Peel the potatoes and cut them into sixths. Add them to the watercress with the water and a pinch of salt. Cook gently, uncovered, for about 15 minutes until tender. Two minutes before the end, add the rest of the watercress. Purée in a blender, then sieve.

Open and shell the oysters, straining their liquor into a saucepan. Heat the oysters in the liquor for about 45 seconds until they begin to firm. Strain and add the liquor to the watercress. Stir in the double cream and taste for seasoning.

Fillets of Fish Wrapped in Lettuce

Divide the watercress cream between 4 soup plates and arrange the oysters in a circle on top. Decorate with sprigs of chervil.

FILLETS OF FISH WRAPPED IN LETTUCE
Serves Four

The Moon favours fish beyond all else and this mode of part baking, part steaming seems well in tune with the planet. A firm fish is preferable, but by no means essential: sole, brill, cod or hake would do very well. Serve with a dish of French beans or, perhaps, some puréed celeriac.

4 oz/125g shallot
5 fl oz/150ml white vermouth
8 large outer leaves of Webb's lettuce
salt and pepper
1¼ lb/550g fillets of fish, skinned
2 tablespoons double cream
lemon juice
2 oz/50g butter, cut in pieces
chervil to decorate

Peel and chop the shallot. Put in a pan with the vermouth and boil, uncovered, to reduce the liquid to 5 tablespoons.

Wash the lettuce leaves and place them in a large pan of salted boiling water for 20 seconds. Refresh under a cold tap and drain. Remove the largest of the ribs from the leaves.

Season the fillets and divide into 4 portions. Flatten out the leaves in overlapping pairs and place the portions of fish in the centre of each pair. Wrap the lettuce around the fish.

Put the reduced vermouth into a fireproof baking dish and place the fish parcels on top. Cover the dish with foil and bake in a preheated oven at 300°F/150°C/Gas Mark 2 for between 5 and 10 minutes or longer, depending on the thickness of the fillet. Remove the fish parcels to a serving dish and keep warm. Put the baking dish over heat and bubble up the juices. Stir in the cream, boil briefly, season with lemon juice and more salt and pepper. Take the dish off the heat and add the butter a piece at a time whisking as you go. Taste and pour round the fish.

CRISPY STEAMED DUCK WITH WATER CHESTNUTS AND MUSHROOMS
Serves Four

Moon food is either boiled or steamed. This Chinese technique of frying *after* steaming makes sure that the skin is nicely crisped. Water chestnuts and mushrooms are the right sort of texture and taste for a lunar meal. The choice of duck is here determined by the lunar preference for waterfowl. Serve with boiled rice.

For the duck
1 tablespoon dry sherry
1 teaspoon soy sauce
1 teaspoon wine vinegar
1 knob preserve stem ginger, chopped
2 teaspoons preserved ginger syrup
pinch five spice powder
salt and black pepper
4 duck breasts, each about 7 oz/200g
4 fl oz/120ml vegetable oil

For the water chestnuts and mushrooms
12 dried black Chinese mushrooms
4 spring onions
4 oz/125g button mushrooms
10 water chestnuts
½ teaspoon grated fresh ginger root
1 teaspoon sherry
1 tablespoon vegetable oil
salt

For the sauce
1 tablespoon oyster sauce
2 teaspoons cornflour mixed with 1 tablespoon cold water
salt and pepper
1 tablespoon vegetable oil

Prepare the marinade by mixing the first 7 ingredients together in a bowl. Rub the duck breasts vigorously with the marinade. Cover the bowl and leave in the refrigerator overnight, turning the duck breasts in the marinade at least once.

Next day cook the vegetables. Soak the Chinese mushrooms in hot water to cover for 30 minutes. Squeeze dry, discard the stalks and slice the mushrooms. Reserve the mushrooms and soaking water.

Slice the spring onions finely, green part as well as white; remove the stalks and quarter the button mushrooms; slice the water chestnuts. Mix the vegetables with the remaining ingredients and put in a heatproof dish. Put a rack in a wok or large pan. Pour in about 2 inches/5cm boiling water. Put the dish on the rack, cover the wok and steam for approximately 12 minutes. Drain and reserve the liquor that has come out during the cooking. Keep the vegetables warm.

Put the duck breasts on a heatproof dish and steam in the same way as the vegetables for approximately 25 minutes until tender. Remove the breasts and keep warm. Save the juices that have flowed during cooking and skim them of their fat.

To make the sauce, put 3 fluid ounces/75ml of the liquor from the vegetables and the skimmed liquor from the duck breasts in a saucepan with the oyster sauce. Add the cornflour and cook gently, uncovered, for 4 minutes to a fine sauce. Taste for seasoning. Stir in the oil, and keep warm while you fry the duck breasts.

Heat the oil in a wok or frying pan to nearly smoking and fry the breasts briskly for 2 minutes on each side.

Put a duck breast on each plate, some of the sauce over one end of the breast, spreading into the rest of the plate. Then put some of the vegetables on top of the pool of sauce. Serve immediately.

MUSHROOMS WITH GARLIC, PARSLEY AND RED WINE
Serves Four

Mushrooms — it's obvious once thought about — are preternaturally lunar. This dish, which can be eaten hot or cool, benefits from the saltiness and tang of bacon. If you wish to eat it without meat, you may find it is improved by the addition of extremely reduced mushroom water obtained from soaking dried mushrooms or ceps which may themselves be added to the pan.

1 lb/450g smallest button mushrooms
2 double thick rashers streaky bacon
2 cloves garlic
3 fl oz/85ml olive oil
salt and black pepper
8 fl oz/250ml red wine
2 tablespoons chopped parsley

Wipe the mushrooms carefully and trim their stalks, do not wash. If they are not the smallest buttons, cut in half; trim the rashers and cut them into small dice; peel and chop the garlic very finely.

In a wide pan or wok, fry the bacon briskly in the oil over high heat until crisp and brown. Add the mushrooms and garlic and continue to fry briskly, tossing and turning, for 2 minutes. Season with a little salt and lots of pepper. Add the red wine and continue turning the mushrooms while bubbling fiercely for 2 minutes. Add the parsley 20 seconds before finishing the cooking.

Remove the mushrooms with a slotted spoon to a dish. Continue boiling the wine until reduced to only 6 tablespoons. Taste for seasoning and pour over the mushrooms. Serve hot or at room temperature.

PICKLED WATERMELON RIND
Makes two pints/1.1 litre

In the Middle and Far East, watermelon rind is treated as a sweetmeat but in America it figures as a pickle — an essential of Pennsylvania Dutch traditional fare or Southern states cooking. The fruit is too large to let it go entirely to waste. So, next time you have a watermelon and have consumed all the bright flesh, think of this way to deal with the rind.

2 lb/900g watermelon rind
4 tablespoons salt
1 lb/450g sugar
12 fl oz/350ml cider vinegar
1 tablespoon allspice
1 teaspoon cloves
1 stick cinnamon
1 tablespoon sliced fresh ginger root

Trim the rind of all its flesh and remove the green skin. Cut the rind into 1 inch/2.5 cm cubes and put in a bowl. Pour over a brine made with the salt and water. Leave overnight.

Drain the melon rind and put in a large pan with plenty of boiling water. Boil for approximately 1 hour. Drain and cool.

Dissolve the sugar in 2 pints/1.1 litres cold water and the vinegar. Add the spices, tied in a muslin bag, and boil for 5 minutes. Add the melon rind and simmer, uncovered, for between 40 and 60 minutes until the rind is transparent. Let it stand overnight.

With a slotted spoon transfer the melon rind to sterilized jars. Return the pan to the heat and cook the syrup, uncovered, for about 30 minutes until it thickens. Pour the syrup over the melon rind, cover tightly and leave for 3 weeks.

DEVONSHIRE JUNKET AND PRUNE WHIP
Serves Four
Junket is an especially English way of setting milk to make a simple and digestible dessert. It uses rennet, also employed for setting the curds for hard cheese. Its suggested partnership with a prune whip makes a suitably low key course for a lunar meal — hardly a time for strong or vibrant tastes.

For the prunes
1 teaspoon Earl Grey tea
1 pint/600ml boiling water
8 oz/225g prunes
1 tablespoon sugar
rind of ½ lemon
juice of ¼ lemon
3 tablespoons whipping cream
For the junket
1 pint/600ml lukewarm milk
1 tablespoon sugar, or to taste
1 tablespoon brandy
3 teaspoons rennet essence
nutmeg

Infuse the tea in the water for 5 minutes. Strain the liquid over the prunes and soak overnight.

Next day put the prunes and tea in a pan with the sugar and lemon rind. Cover and boil gently until tender. Drain and stone the prunes. Push them through a sieve into a bowl. Add the lemon juice and cool completely.

Whip the cream until stiff and fold into the prunes. Taste and add more sugar if necessary. Cover and put in the refrigerator to chill.

Heat the milk to lukewarm; do not let it boil. Add the sugar and dissolve. Add the brandy and the rennet essence. Put in a bowl, cover and leave in a warm place, without stirring, for 30 minutes until set. Grate nutmeg over the top. Do not chill.

Serve the junket and prune whip in separate bowls, allowing guests to help themselves.

MELON AND LOGANBERRIES IN MUSCAT WINE
Serves Four
This will only be really fantastic if everything is ripe, especially the loganberries which need to be their darkest hue before they give of their best flavour. The melon must be from the most fragrant varieties. Serve by itself or with cream.
1 melon, Charentais or Ogen
2 tablespoons sugar
7 fl oz/200ml Muscat de Beaumes de Venise or de Frontignan
12 oz/350g loganberries
mint leaves

Seed the melon. Take out the flesh in balls with a melon scoop and put in a bowl. Sprinkle with 1 tablespoon of the sugar and pour in the wine. Put the loganberries in another bowl and sprinkle with the remaining sugar.

Cover both bowls with clingfilm and leave to macerate in the refrigerator. Just before serving gently mix the melon with the loganberries. The loganberry juice will impart a blush to the melon.

MERCURY

RULER OF GEMINI AND VIRGO

MERCURY is the planet of thought, ideas and communication and is a lover of change and variety. It rules recipe books, and Mercurial people are likely to be experimental in their choice of food. They think a lot about what they eat and can be quite fussy. They are also inclined to eat too quickly, or to read while eating, and are often to be found sitting at the table with a book or magazine.

MERCURY ENVIRONMENTS
Mercury is a lively and interesting planet and rules all educational establishments, libraries, television and newspaper offices.

MERCURY COOKING
Fast food and rapid methods of cooking.

MERCURY FOOD
Light, varied and interesting, Mercury food contains a mixture of many different ingredients. Mercury is associated with the quality of taste in general, but the flavour of its foods are often overwhelmed by those of the more powerful planets. Flavour enhancers which complement food while having no particular taste of their own are ruled by this sign. Mercurial food is often cold and dry. Mercurial plants are said to play a medicinal role in removing obstructions.

MERCURY MEAT, FISH AND POULTRY
As Mercury rules all animals which are fast runners it is associated with venison. Other meats include tongue; fish include mullet.

MERCURY VEGETABLES, GRAINS ETC.
Fennel, carrots, celery, beans, oats and grains in general.

MERCURY FRUITS AND NUTS
Except for mulberry, hazelnut and walnut, no fruits and nuts are ruled by Mercury.

MERCURY HERBS, SPICES AND FLAVOURINGS, ETC.
Parsley, dill, vervain, fennel seed, caraway, fenugreek, liquorice, marjoram and savory.

AVOCADO MOUSSE WITH THREE SAUCES
Serves Four

Mercury likes food of variety, the multiple sauces and colours of modern cooking thus appeal.

For the mousse
3 ripe avocados
2 oz/50g butter, melted
10 fl oz/300ml sour cream
juice of ½ lemon
salt and pepper
3 egg whites
1 tablespoon chopped chives

For the tomato sauce
4 tomatoes
2 tablespoons wine vinegar
salt and pepper
sugar
2 tablespoons olive oil

For the red pepper sauce
3 canned red peppers
¼ teaspoon *harissa* — N. African chilli paste
1 tablespoon wine vinegar
salt
2 tablespoons olive oil

For the carrot sauce
4 carrots
salt
1 tablespoon orange juice
1 teaspoon vinegar
pepper
3 tablespoons olive oil

Halve the avocados and remove their flesh. Put it in a blender with the melted butter, sour cream, lemon juice and seasoning. Blend to a purée and put into a bowl. Whisk the egg whites stiffly and fold into the avocado purée, together with the chopped chives. Leave covered in the refrigerator for at least 2 hours.

Peel, seed and chop the tomatoes into a blender with the vinegar and seasoning. Blend, pouring in the oil in a thin stream. Chill.

Put the peppers, *harissa*, vinegar and seasoning into a blender and blend, pouring in the oil as before. Chill.

Peel the carrots and cut into 4 lengthwise. Cook in boiling salted water for 15 minutes. Drain and put in a blender with the orange juice, vinegar, more salt, if necessary, and pepper. Blend until completely smooth, adding the oil as before. Chill.

Cover the bottom of 4 cold plates with the sauces, keeping the lines between them crisp and definite. Using spoons dipped in hot water, arrange spoonfuls of the mousse in the centre.

LOIN OF LAMB COATED WITH MUSHROOMS
Serves Four

This is another variation on the theme of food as a flavour enhancer: the identity of the mushrooms being merged with that of the lamb. The parsley accompaniment is a second example of putting the herb centre stage. This is a dish of small portions, but lamb is always more substantial than it appears. Try serving soufflé potatoes with it and, if you think it necessary, a bowl of garden peas to go with the best of spring lamb.

8 noisettes of lamb, each about 3 oz/75g, about
    1½ inches/4cm thick, trimmed of skin,
    membrane and fat.
salt and black pepper
3 oz/75g mushrooms
1 egg
1 oz/25g butter
1 tablespoon oil

For the parsley
4 bunches parsley
1 shallot
salt
2 oz/50g butter
5 fl oz/150ml double cream
black pepper
lemon juice

First prepare the parsley by cutting off the coarse stems; peel and chop the shallot. Drop the parsley into a large pan of boiling salted water and boil, uncovered, for approximately 2 minutes. Drain and dry very well.

Heat the butter in a frying pan and fry the shallot

for about 3 minutes or until transparent but not coloured. Add the parsley and fry for 1 minute longer. Add the cream and boil, stirring, for 2 minutes. Season, adding lemon juice if necessary. Keep hot.

Season the lamb. Chop the mushrooms extremely fine — but not to a purée — and spread them on a plate. Beat the egg. Dip the noisettes in the egg then roll them in the mushrooms to coat.

Melt the butter with the oil. Sear the lamb on both sides over high heat. Put, uncovered, in a preheated oven at 425°F/220°C/Gas Mark 7 for 4 minutes. Remove and leave to rest in a warm place for 3 minutes.

Put the lamb on a serving dish. Arrange the parsley around the lamb and serve.

PHEASANT BRAISED WITH CELERY AND PORT
Serves Six

Mercury being so changeable — mercurial indeed — it has few specific ingredients linked to its name. Celery is an exception and is here shown to best advantage with this casserole of pheasant, a way

Liquorice Gingerbread

to make a slightly tough bird go down well. A pheasant usually sufficient for three people — getting four portions can mean stretching. Thus I have given quantities for two birds. If in the winter, serve this with Brussel sprouts cooked with hazelnuts and a potato purée.

2 pheasants, ready to cook
salt and black pepper
1 head celery
3 oz/75g butter
4 oz/125g salt pork or streaky bacon, diced
3 fl oz/85ml brandy
10 fl oz/300ml ruby port
6 fl oz/175ml pheasant or chicken stock
1 tablespoon redcurrant jelly
5 fl oz/150ml double cream

Season the pheasants inside and out. Trim, wash and rid the celery of its strings. Cut into matchsticks. Melt the butter in a large casserole and fry the diced bacon. Add the pheasants and brown well on all sides. Warm the brandy, set it alight and pour over the birds. When the flames subside remove the pheasants from the casserole and set aside.

Put the celery in the casserole and cook, covered, over gentle heat for about 15 minutes until tender. Replace the pheasants, breasts downwards. Add the port and stock and bring to the boil. Turn the heat to the lowest and simmer, covered, until cooked. This may take anything from 40 to 90 minutes depending on the toughness of the birds.

Remove the pheasants and carve into joints. Arrange on a large flameproof dish. With a slotted spoon transfer the celery to the dish. Keep covered.

Put the casserole back on the heat and boil rapidly to reduce the liquid by half. Add the redcurrant jelly and the cream. Stir to dissolve then boil to reduce by half again. Taste for seasoning. Pour the sauce over the pheasant and reheat gently.

AUBERGINE AND PARSNIP CRISPS
Serves Four
More mercurial variety here with crisps not from potato but two different sorts of vegetable that offer a contrast of sweet and slightly bitter in the same dish. It is best if the aubergine is not too large, with too loose a centre. Also, the parsnip should never be so large as to be woody at the core. These will go well with game or any grilled meat with a concentrated sauce.

1 aubergine
2 medium parsnips
4 oz/125g seasoned flour
salt
oil for deep frying

Cut the aubergine in half lengthwise. Cut into thin slices and sprinkle with salt in a colander. Leave to drain under a weighted plate for 30 minutes. Rinse and dry very well with a paper towel. Scrub and trim the parsnips very well but try to avoid peeling them. Cut them into very thin slices. Put the seasoned flour on a tray and turn the aubergine slices in it.

Heat the oil to 375°F/190°C and fry both vegetables in small batches for about 2 minutes until golden. Keep the slices separate and turn them if necessary with a long fork. Do not let the oil overheat. Drain on paper towels and season before serving immediately.

LIQUORICE GINGERBREAD
Makes one 8 inch/20cm square cake
One of Mercury's spices is liquorice, not used much for cooking today, though found often enough in candy and sweet drinks. Its digestive properties must account for its connection to this planet. In the Middle Ages it was used in the making of gingerbread and I have suggested it here as a substitute for mixed spice in a sticky gingerbread for eating at tea-time. Liquorice root may be bought from herbalists. It is ground before use.

2 oz/50g butter plus extra for the cake tin
2 oz/50g brown sugar
3 tablespoons black treacle
6 oz/175g plain flour
2 teaspoons baking powder
2 teaspoons ground ginger
1 teaspoon ground liquorice root

pinch salt
3 eggs, beaten
7 fl oz/200ml milk
1 teaspoon bicarbonate of soda

Grease an 8 inch/20cm square cake tin with butter.

In a bowl, cream the butter, sugar and treacle. Sift the flour, baking powder, spices and salt into the bowl and beat well. Add the eggs. Warm the milk, dissolve the bicarbonate in it and add that to the mixture. Beat until it starts to bubble slightly. Pour into the cake tin. Bake in a preheated oven at 325°F/160°C/Gas Mark 3 for about 1 hour, or until a knife inserted into the centre comes out clean. Leave the gingerbread undisturbed for the first 40 minutes in the oven.

Take the cake out of the oven and leave to cool in the tin. When cool, turn the gingerbread out and store it in a container and do not eat for 24 hours.

A LAYERED ICE CREAM CAKE
Serves at least Six
More variety for Mercury, this time something allied to another of Mercury's favourites — fast food. The ice cream here is made in layers as is a Neapolitan. This makes it very difficult to make without an ice cream machine for you need the volume it gives you and the layers cannot be disturbed once they have been made. Make it in a 2 pint/1.1 litre china soufflé dish, or round cake tin, which is lined with clingfilm to ease the unmoulding of the finished dessert.

For the honey and cardamom ice cream
3 cardamom pods
5 fl oz/150ml milk
3 fl oz/85ml honey
1 egg yolk
3 fl oz/85ml double cream
For the hazelnut ice cream
2 oz/50g hazelnuts
7 fl oz/200ml milk
1 egg yolk
1 tablespoon sugar

For the chocolate ice cream
3 oz/75g plain chocolate
6 fl oz/175ml single cream
1 egg yolk
2 tablespoons sugar
For decoration
1 oz/25g peeled unsalted pistachio nuts

Put the cardamom and milk in a pan and bring to the boil. Infuse off the heat for 20 minutes. Strain the milk and mix with the honey. Return to the pan and bring to the boil. In a bowl whisk the egg and cream together very well. Pour on the scalded, but not boiling, milk and honey. Set the bowl over a pan of hot water on low heat and cook, stirring, for about 7 minutes or until the mixture coats the back of the spoon. Strain the custard and cool completely. Churn in the ice cream machine. Spread as a bottom layer in the mould. Cover the mould and leave in the freezer.

Roast the hazelnuts in the oven at 325°F/160°C/Gas Mark 3 for about 5 to 10 minutes until slightly browned. Rub their skins off. Scald the milk. Put the nuts and milk in a blender and blend for 2 minutes. Set aside to cool.

Strain the milk, pressing through every bit of goodness. In a bowl, beat the egg yolk and sugar together until pale. Add the milk and set the bowl over a pan of hot water on low heat. Cook, stirring, for about 12 minutes or until the mixture coats the back of the spoon. Cool completely. Churn in the ice cream machine. Spread as the next layer and return to the freezer.

In a bowl set over a pan of hot water on low heat, melt the chocolate in the cream. Whisk the egg yolk and sugar together until pale and stir into the hot chocolate and cream. Cook for about 7 minutes or until the mixture coats the back of the spoon. Cool completely. Churn and add as the last layer to the mould. Return to the freezer and leave for at least 2 hours.

To serve, unmould the ice cream. Leave it in the refrigerator for about 30 to 45 minutes to come up to serving temperature. Decorate with pistachio nuts.

VENUS

RULER OF TAURUS AND LIBRA

VENUS is the softest and most feminine of all the planets. In the ancient world it was worshipped as the goddess of love. Although its general nature is passive it is easily roused to passion. Venus is the ruler of the arts, beauty and all sensual pleasures.

VENUS ENVIRONMENTS

These should be peaceful, pleasing and soothing to the senses. Gardens, especially those containing sweet smelling herbs and flowers are ruled by Venus, as are dancing schools, bridal chambers and bedrooms. The Venusian dinner should above all be romantic, with a mood set by sensitive lighting and music.

VENUS COOKING

Venus is a moderately cold, moist planet, so it is associated with salads. Boiling and poaching are the preferred methods of cooking and the food is often, though not always, served cold.

VENUS FOOD

Venus food is always well presented, with an emphasis on appearance rather than substance. It calms the spirit and has an amorous and aphrodisiac quality. It is moderately rich often cooked with cream, liqueurs or other alcohol. Venus rules the sense of smell in general and therefore all sweet smelling and perfumed fruit which are sweet and juicy.

VENUS MEAT, FISH AND POULTRY

Venison, veal, beef, goat, chicken, partridge, grouse, pheasant, rabbit, lobster, salmon and sardines.

VENUS VEGETABLES, GRAINS, ETC

Artichokes, asparagus, sorrel, parsnips, beans, buckwheat, rye, millet and wheat.

VENUS FRUIT AND NUTS

Venus is the ruler of fruit in general, but specifically of apples, all currants, oranges, pears, figs, peaches, apricots, plums, raisins, cherries, grapes, mangoes, dates, gooseberries, strawberries, raspberries and olives. Venus is also associated with walnuts.

VENUS HERBS, SPICES AND FLAVOURINGS, ETC

Venus is especially linked to savoury herbs including thyme, coriander, origano, fenugreek, cloves, peppermint, parsley, vervain and yarrow.

COLD ALMOND SOUP, WITH GARLIC, BROAD BEANS AND PARSLEY

Serves Four

4 oz/125g almonds
3 cloves garlic
salt
1 slice white bread, crust removed
6 fl oz/175ml olive oil
1 fl oz/25ml sherry or white wine vinegar
1 pint/600ml ice-cold water
4 oz/125g very young shelled broad beans
1 bunch parsley

Blanch the almonds, skin them and chop them roughly. In a mortar pound the garlic with a good pinch of salt. Soak the bread in water, squeeze dry and add to the mortar with the almonds. Continue to pound until reduced to a paste. Alternatively, use a blender or food processor.

Add the oil drop by drop to the paste, beating all the time to attain an emulsion. Then add the vinegar likewise. Transfer to a soup tureen and slowly add the water. Check the seasoning.

Put the broad beans in a small pan. Just cover with water and simmer gently for 5 to 10 minutes or until tender. If the beans are not as young as they should be, remove the skins. Drain the beans and refresh in cold water. Add the beans to the soup. Chop the parsley and stir it in. Chill the soup before serving.

TARTS OF ARTICHOKES WITH A SOUFFLE TOPPING

Serves Four

Serve with a salad of lamb's lettuce dressed with a vinaigrette.

4 shortcrust pastry cases, each about 4 inches/
    10cm in diameter
2 or 3 globe artichokes
wine vinegar
lemon juice
2 oz/50g butter
salt and white pepper
4 egg whites
4 oz/125g Cheddar cheese, grated

Prick the bottoms of the pastry cases with a fork, line them with aluminium foil and weigh down with dried beans or rice. Bake in a preheated oven at 425°F/220°C/Gas Mark 7 for 20 minutes.

Boil the artichokes in water with a splash of vinegar for upwards of 45 minutes until tender (test with a knife into the heart of the globe). Drain and cool. Discard the outer leaves. Remove the other leaves one by one and scrape off the small bit of tender flesh at the base with the back of a knife. Discard the leaves. Remove the choke at the centre and retain the heart. Squeeze in some lemon juice to prevent discoloration. Put all through the fine plate of a food mill. Put the purée in a small saucepan with the butter, add seasoning and heat through.

Put the pastry cases on a baking sheet. Fill with the artichoke purée. Whisk the egg whites until they form firm peaks and fold in three-quarters of the cheese. Pile the egg whites on top of the purée, sprinkle the remaining cheese on top and bake in a preheated oven at 400°F/200°C/Gas Mark 6 for about 10 minutes or until golden brown. Serve immediately.

WILD DUCK WITH GINGER AND PORT

Serves Four

2 wild mallard, or if more convenient, 4 breasts
    of barbary or muscovy duck
salt and pepper
oil
1 shallot
3 pieces preserved stem ginger
1 tablespoon stem ginger syrup
3 fl oz/85ml port
8 fl oz/250ml poultry or game stock
2 teaspoons grated fresh ginger root
lemon juice
5 fl oz/150ml double cream

Season the ducks. Heat a little oil in a frying pan and sear the ducks, turning them to brown all over. Transfer them to a roasting pan and roast in a preheated oven at 450°F/230°C/Gas Mark 8 for about 20 minutes. Remove the ducks from the pan

Tarts of Artichokes with a Souffle Topping

and keep warm. If using duck breasts, sear on both sides then cook in the oven for approximately 7 minutes.

Meanwhile, chop the shallot and the stem ginger. Put the ginger syrup, port, stock and shallot in a saucepan and bring to the boil. Continue boiling until the liquid is reduced by half. Add the chopped stem ginger, the grated fresh ginger and juice from a wedge of lemon. Continue cooking until the sauce becomes syrupy then add the cream and cook until it has a coating consistency. Taste for seasoning.

Carve the duck, arranging the breasts and legs on a heated dish, pour sauce round them and serve immediately.

PHEASANT BRAISED WITH PLUMS
Serves Three

This is a classic Venusian combination of game with fruit, flavouring calculated to warm your heart in the colourful days of late autumn. Serve with potato griddle cakes (see page 17) and a celeriac purée.

1 young dressed pheasant, about 1¾ lb/800g
salt and pepper

2 rashers streaky bacon
1 small onion
2 oz/50g butter
1½ fl oz/40ml armagnac brandy, or, better still,
    eau de vie de quetsch
12 large plums, halved and stoned
4 fl oz/120ml white wine
1 tablespoon redcurrant jelly
2 oz/50g butter, cut in pieces
ground allspice

Rub the pheasant with salt and pepper. Dice the bacon; peel and chop the onion. In a casserole, melt the butter and fry the bacon and onion until lightly browned. Add the pheasant and brown each side of the breast. Leave it on its side. Warm the armagnac in a small pan, set it alight and pour it over the bird. When the flames subside, cover the casserole and cook gently for 25 minutes. Turn the bird over, add the plums and continue cooking for a further 20 minutes.

Transfer the pheasant and the plums to a heated dish and keep warm while you finish the sauce. Drain off some of the fat from the pan and add the white wine. Boil fiercely to reduce the sauce. Stir in the redcurrant jelly and when it has dissolved, whisk in the butter piece by piece. Adjust the seasoning, using some ground allspice as well as salt and pepper.

A CHICKPEA, TOMATO AND ONION SALAD WITH YOGHURT
Serves Four
14 oz/400g tin chickpeas
1 clove garlic
4 tablespoons olive oil
½ tablespoon ground cumin
4 oz/125g tin tomato purée
1 bunch parsley, chopped
salt
1 onion
milk
seasoned flour
olive oil
15 oz/425g sheep's milk yoghurt

Drain the chickpeas, rinse and drain well. Peel and chop the garlic and put it in a small pan with the oil, cumin and tomato purée. Cook, stirring briskly, until the cumin smells strongly. Take the pan off the heat and add the chickpeas together with most of the parsley and seasoning. Return to the heat to coat the chickpeas with the tomato mixture, then set aside.

Peel and slice the onion into thin rings. Dip into milk then dredge with seasoned flour. Heat some olive oil in a frying pan and fry the onion rings until well browned. Put the chickpeas on a serving dish, scatter the onion rings over the top and surround with a ring of yoghurt. Scatter the rest of the parsley on the yoghurt.

A SEMISWEET TART OF SPINACH, RAISINS AND PINE KERNELS
Serves Four
2 oz/50g raisins
2 fl oz/50ml dark rum
1 lb/450g spinach
2 oz/50g butter
1 oz/25g mild Cheddar cheese
1 egg
2 oz/50g brown sugar
2 oz/50g pine kernels
shortcrust pastry made with 8 oz/225g flour
eggwash made with ½ egg and a little milk
caster sugar
cream for serving

In a large bowl, soak the raisins in the rum for 1 hour.

Strip, wash well and drain the spinach. Cook in the butter in a covered pan for about 5 minutes, stirring frequently. Drain well and chop.

Grate the cheese, beat the egg and add to the raisins along with the brown sugar and pine kernels. Mix in the cooled spinach.

Line a 10 inch/25cm tart tin or flan dish with the pastry. Prick the bottom with a fork, line with aluminium foil, weigh down with dried beans and bake in a preheated oven at 425°F/220°C/Gas Mark 7 for 8 minutes.

Fill the pastry shell with the spinach mixture. With the pastry trimmings make a criss-cross lattice over the top. Brush with the eggwash and sprinkle with caster sugar. Bake in a preheated oven at 350°F/180°C/Gas Mark 4 for approximately 30 minutes. Serve with cream.

STRAWBERRY AND ROSE PETAL ICE CREAM
Serves Four

A delicate and beautiful ice cream confection coloured with the heartfelt fervour of the old-fashioned red rose — a suitable presentation for your dearest friends.

1 large old-fashioned red rose
1 lb/450g ripe strawberries
8 oz/225g caster sugar
juice of ½ lemon
10 fl oz/300ml double cream

Strip the petals from the rose; hull the strawberries. Purée the fruit, petals, sugar and lemon juice in a blender. Lightly whip the cream and fold it into the purée. Pour the mixture into a container, cover and freeze.

After 2 hours or when the mixture is just beginning to set, remove it from the freezer, tip into a bowl and beat well. Return to the freezer and repeat once more after 1 hour. Freeze for at least 4 hours before serving.

WINTER FRUIT SALAD IN RED WINE
Serves Four

8 prunes
8 dried apricots
2 oz/50g sultanas
2 large cooking pears
1 small orange
½ stick cinnamon
good pinch allspice
½ vanilla pod
3 oz/75g caster sugar
½ bottle red wine
10 walnut halves
Chantilly cream
sponge fingers

Soak the prunes, apricots and sultanas in water for 30 minutes, then drain. Peel and quarter the pears; take the zest off a quarter of the orange with a potato peeler, omitting any pith; peel and segment the rest of the orange.

In a small casserole arrange the dried fruit and pears. Add the spices, vanilla pod, sugar and orange zest and put the orange segments over the top. Pour on the wine and cook gently, just simmering, for 30 minutes.

When cool, remove the cinnamon and vanilla pod. Arrange the walnut halves on top. Serve with Chantilly cream and sponge fingers.

MUSCAT GRAPES IN A MUSCAT JELLY
Serves Four

A confection straight from the dreams of Bacchus.

½ oz/15g (1 sachet) powdered gelatine
4 oz/125g sugar
8 fl oz/250ml water
8 fl oz/250ml muscat wine, e.g. Muscat de Beaumes de Venise or Muscat de Frontignan
12 oz/350g ripe muscat grapes

Put the gelatine and 4 tablespoons of water in a cup and leave to soften. Put the sugar and water in a saucepan over low heat and stir to dissolve. Stir in the wine. Taste to check that the sweetness is to your liking. Add the gelatine to the syrup while still warm but not boiling hot and stir until the gelatine is dissolved. Leave to cool.

Skin the grapes and remove their pips. Pour about half the liquid into a bowl or mould. Arrange the fruit on top when it starts to set. Pour on the remainder of the liquid and set in the refrigerator.

MARS

RULER OF ARIES AND SCORPIO

MARS is the most energetic and active of the planets, and its hot, fiery disposition has long been associated with power and aggression. It is impatient, and loves to lead and take control. In the ancient world Mars was venerated as the god of war.

MARS ENVIRONMENTS

Favourite Martian surroundings are stimulating, colourful, lively, energetic and noisy. They are also likely to be crowded and hot; a discotheque is typical. Plush red fittings are appropriate; bright lights are likely. In the kitchen Mars rules the stove.

MARS COOKING

Because Mars is extremely hot and dry, it rules such methods of cooking as baking, toasting, grilling, roasting and barbecuing. This is an impatient planet and is, therefore, also connected with food which can be prepared or eaten very quickly. For example, stir-fried or 'fast food' is ruled by this planet (together with Mercury), so is food which is mashed or puréed. Much Mars food is also characterized by the colour red.

MARS FOODS

Hot, dry, spicy, pungent and bitter, although not necessarily all at the same time, many Mars foods agitate and stimulate the senses.

MARS FISH, MEAT AND POULTRY

Shark, pike and goat are all ruled by Mars.

MARS VEGETABLES, GRAINS, ETC

Mars plants are characterized by spiky leaves and/or a hot taste and tend to grow in dry places. Vegetables include capsicums, nettles, onion, garlic, radish, leeks and aubergine.

MARS FRUITS AND NUTS

Mars is not normally associated with fruits, although it rules the pineapple and other fruits which have spiky skins. Rhubarb comes under its influence because of its red colour.

MARS HERBS, SPICES AND FLAVOURINGS, ETC

Mars rules all hot and stimulating herbs and spices including garlic, pepper, ginger, mustard, chilli, basil, capsicum, capers, cayenne, tamarind and horseradish as well as tea, coffee, tobacco and hops.

TOMATO AND RED PEPPER SOUP
Serves Four

This hits the Martian theme with two barrels — tomatoes *and* red peppers. Much of the planet's menu, indeed, is a contemplation of this combination. This soup goes well with garlic croûtons.

6 tomatoes
3 teaspoons wine vinegar
2 teaspoons sugar
1 large onion
2 large red peppers
2 sweetcorn cobs
2 tablespoons olive oil
2 pints/1.1 litres chicken stock
pinch saffron
good pinch cayenne pepper
1 teaspoon paprika
salt
chopped parsley for decorating

Chop the tomatoes coarsely. Put them in a pan with the vinegar and sugar and boil for about 4 minutes to evaporate nearly all the liquid. Sieve to make a purée.

Peel and chop the onion; grill or roast the peppers until their skins are charred and blistered. Skin under cold water. Halve, remove seeds and stalk and cut into small dice; strip the corn off the cobs, using a knife to cut down close to the cob.

Heat the oil in a saucepan and fry the onion gently for 5 minutes until transparent. Add the tomato purée, peppers, corn and stock and bring to the boil. Season with saffron, cayenne and paprika. Cook uncovered for about 12 minutes or until the corn is tender. Season with salt. Serve immediately, sprinkling parsley on top.

SHARK WITH LEMON
Serves Four

Mars is not associated with fish except for those peculiarly violent types — the shark and the pike. In fact, the shark most often caught in northern waters, the porbeagle, is fairly equable, certainly to man. Its flesh resembles nothing so much as veal.

Serve it, to remain Martian, with two purées — of broccoli and carrots — and some fried potatoes.

zest and juice of ½ lemon
4 escalopes of shark, each about 5 oz/150g
salt and pepper
4 oz/125g butter
4 fl oz/120ml white wine
2 teaspoons wine vinegar
½ teaspoon leaves of lemon thyme
1 lemon cut in wedges for serving

Take the zest off the lemon with a potato peeler, without any pith. Blanch in boiling water for 2 minutes. Drain, then reboil in fresh water. Repeat. Cut into the finest strips and reserve.

Season the shark with salt, pepper and the lemon juice. Melt half the butter in a large pan and fry the shark escalopes quickly on both sides for about 3 minutes to brown; the time will depend on the thickness of the slices but do not let them become dry. Lift out the escalopes and keep warm.

Put the wine and vinegar into the pan over high heat and boil to reduce by half. Add the lemon strips and the lemon thyme. Taste for seasoning. Whisk in the remaining butter. There will only be a little strong sauce for each person. Serve with lemon wedges.

BARBECUED PORK TEX-MEX
Serves Four

The cooking of Mars suits the cuisine of Mexico and southwestern USA which makes such creative use of the chilli and pimento. This dish can be fiery. Serve it with a salad — tomatoes and greens — and some crisp sauté potatoes.

For the meat
4 cloves garlic
6 green chillis
1 canned red pepper
1 teaspoon marjoram
½ teaspoon ground cumin
good pinch ground cinnamon
½ teaspoon salt
6 fl oz/175ml water
3 tablespoons vinegar

1½ lb/700g pork tenderloin
ground nutoil for brushing
For the red salsa
2 rashers streaky bacon
1 onion
1 clove garlic
1 red chilli
1 red pepper
1 tablespoon oil
14 oz/400g can tomatoes
salt
cayenne pepper, optional
sugar to taste
For the avocado
4 avocados
lemon juice
1 green chilli
1 tablespoon wine vinegar
6 tablespoons groundnut oil
1 tablespoon Dijon mustard
salt

First make a marinade. Peel the garlic and remove the stalks of the chillis. Put them in a blender with the red pepper, herb, spices, salt, water and vinegar. Blend to a purée.

Trim the pork of all membranes and fat. Cut into 1 inch/2.5cm cubes. Thread onto skewers and put in a dish. Spoon the marinade over them. Keep in the marinade, turning regularly, for at least 12 hours.

To make the salsa dice the bacon; peel and chop the onion and garlic; remove the stalk and chop the chilli; seed and chop the pepper. Heat the oil in a saucepan and fry the bacon for 2 minutes. Add the onion and fry for 4 minutes. Add the garlic and fry for 1 minute. Add the chilli and pepper and cook, uncovered, for 5 minutes. Add the tomatoes and boil for about 2 minutes to reduce the liquid. Season with salt, cayenne, if desired, and a pinch of sugar. Keep hot.

Next, halve and peel the avocados. Slice 3 of them into long thin slices and arrange on a dish. Brush with lemon juice and cover with clingfilm to stop discolouring. Seed the chilli. Put the other

avocado in the blender with the chilli, vinegar, oil and mustard. Blend to a purée. Taste for seasoning. Pour in a central line down the sliced avocado.

When ready to serve, heat the grill to high or, better, have your charcoal grill red hot. Shake any excess marinade from the meat and grill fast, about 3 minutes on either side. Serve with the salsa and the avocados.

SWEETCORN WITH PIMENTO
Serves Four
4 sweetcorn cobs
1 oz/25g butter
5 fl oz/150ml milk
5 fl oz/150ml double cream
1 egg
pinch sugar
salt
1 green chilli
½ red pepper

Strip the grains off the cobs, making sure you scrape really hard to extract the starchy juices. Melt the butter in a saucepan and sauté the corn for 4 minutes over medium heat. Add the milk and cream. Beat the egg with sugar and salt and stir in to amalgamate. Cook, uncovered, over very gentle heat, stirring, for about 12 minutes.

Remove the stalk and seeds from the green chilli and chop finely; dice the red pepper finely. Add to the pan, continue to cook for 3 to 5 minutes. Taste for seasoning.

NEW WORLD RATATOUILLE
Serves Four
A vegetable mélange that makes a pleasing accompaniment to many dishes but is equally good to eat on its own.
1 onion
1 clove garlic
1 green pepper
1 red pepper
6 oz/175g French beans
4 oz/125g frozen sweetcorn

4 courgettes
2 tomatoes
2 fl oz/50ml olive oil
4 fl oz/120ml chicken or vegetable stock
1 teaspoon chopped fresh coriander
salt and pepper

Peel and slice the onion thinly; peel and chop the garlic; seed and quarter the peppers and slice thinly; top and tail the beans and cut them in thirds or halves; defrost the sweetcorn; wipe and trim the courgettes and cut into fine matchsticks; peel and seed the tomatoes and chop coarsely.

Heat the oil in a saucepan and fry the onion and garlic for 2 minutes without colouring. Add the peppers and beans and cook, uncovered, for a further 4 minutes. Add the corn and courgettes and continue cooking for 2 minutes. Add the tomatoes, stock and coriander and bring to the boil. Simmer for 3 to 5 minutes. Season with salt and pepper. Serve immediately.

CHERRIES WITH A RASPBERRY FOOL
Serves Four
Mars is red and, the rhyme has it, cherries are too. This is a simple summer alliance, but serve it cool rather than cold.

Cherries with a Raspberry Food

For the raspberries
8 oz/225g fresh raspberries
2 oz/50g sugar
8 fl oz/250ml whipping cream
juice of ¼ lemon or to taste

For the cherries
10 fl oz/300ml red wine
4 oz/125g sugar
2 teaspoons redcurrant jelly
pinch cinnamon
1 lb/450g cherries
almond biscuits for serving

Mash the raspberries with the sugar. Whip the cream until firm but not stiff. Fold the cream into the raspberries. Add the lemon juice to taste.

Put the wine, sugar, redcurrant jelly and cinnamon in a small pan. Heat to dissolve the sugar and boil for about 5 minutes, uncovered, to reduce very slightly. Add the cherries and poach gently, uncovered, for about 10 minutes. Stop before they start to wrinkle. Lift out the cherries with a slotted spoon. Continue to reduce the syrup by boiling fast for about 5 minutes. The syrup should be quite thick. Stone the cherries and leave to cool in the syrup.

Layer the raspberry fool and cherry compote in tall glasses and serve with almond biscuits.

COFFEE FLAN WITH A CHOCOLATE SAUCE
Serves Four to Six

Coffee is another Martian commodity, here used in a Hispanic-style custard. There are many Latin American and Spanish desserts that depend on the reduction of milk; this is also found in some Indian recipes. This coffee caramel cream uses modern technology to achieve something of this effect — canned unsweetened evaporated milk. The result is fairly rich.

For the caramel
3 oz/75g sugar

For the custard
10 fl oz/300ml milk
10 fl oz/300ml unsweetened evaporated milk
2 teaspoons instant coffee
2 whole eggs plus 2 egg yolks
2 oz/50g caster sugar
2 tablespoons Tia Maria or Kahlua

For the sauce
3 oz/75g bitter chocolate
2 oz/50g sugar
pinch ground cinnamon
10 fl oz/300ml water

Melt the sugar in a heavy pan until it turns dark golden brown. Pour into a 2 pound/900g loaf tin to cover the bottom. Leave to cool.

In a saucepan, mix the milks and set them to heat. When they get near boiling, whisk in the coffee. Separate the 2 eggs. Beat the four yolks with the sugar in a bowl. Pour on the hot milk, stirring. Add the liqueur. Whisk the egg whites to a stiff peak and stir into the custard. Pour into the loaf tin.

Cover the loaf tin with aluminium foil and put it in a baking dish. Pour in enough hot water to come two-thirds up the sides of the loaf tin. Put the baking dish in an oven preheated to 350°F/180°C/Gas Mark 4 and bake for 45 to 60 minutes or until just set and a knife inserted into the centre comes out clean. Leave to cool completely.

To make the sauce, put the chocolate, sugar and cinnamon in a pan with half the water over gentle heat. When melted, bring to the boil, add the remaining water and simmer uncovered for 10 to 15 minutes until thickened. Let the sauce cool — it can be served either warm or cool but not cold.

To unmould the flan, free the edge with your fingers and invert onto a dish. Serve with the sauce.

JUPITER

RULER OF SAGITTARIUS AND PISCES

JUPITER is an adventurous, optimistic and extrovert planet. In one form it rules physical adventure and exploration, in another it embodies religious beliefs and ideals. It loves liberty and hates limitations or restrictions of any kind. In classical times Jupiter was revered as the king of the gods.

JUPITER ENVIRONMENTS
Richly decorated, comfortable, colourful and luxurious, the Jupiter dining room is a pleasure to eat in. The table is beautifully and extravagantly laid as Jupiterians like to flaunt their wealth. When eating out they usually choose the best restaurants.

JUPITER COOKING
Jupiter is warm and moist, suggesting that food should be roasted or steamed.

JUPITER FOOD
Colourful and lavish, Jupiter food is rich and delicious rather than healthy and Jupiterians are liable to overeat. Jupiter rules banquets, especially religious feasts, for example, weddings and barmitzvahs. The food tends to be sweet or bitter-sweet, well scented and fragrant with rich sauces and is often overcooked.

JUPITER MEAT, FISH AND POULTRY
Jupiter is associated with lamb, venison, partridge, pheasant, chicken, pigeon and all large fish. Liver is also ruled by Jupiter.

JUPITER VEGETABLES, GRAINS, ETC
Asparagus, chicory, endives, parsnips, tomatoes, turnips and leeks all come under Jupiter as do wheat, barley, rice, chickpeas, sesame seed and sugar cane.

JUPITER FRUITS AND NUTS
These include apricots, bilberries, currants, raisins, gooseberries, apples, rhubarb and strawberries.

JUPITER HERBS, SPICES AND FLAVOURINGS, ETC
These are typically sweet smelling and include aniseed, cinnamon, cloves, mint, nutmeg and thyme.

BANANA CURRY SOUP

Serves Four

This soup has something of the rich sweetness allied to Jupiter tastes. Yet, it works extremely satisfactorily, however weird it sounds. It is also a sure-fire way of using up overripe bananas when you have bought too large a hand.

1 lb/450g bananas
1 tablespoon lemon juice
4 oz/125g onion
1 oz/25g butter
1 teaspoon flour
2 scant teaspoons curry powder
1½ pints/900ml chicken stock
salt and black pepper
2 fl oz/50ml double cream
1 tablespoon chopped fresh coriander

Peel the bananas and blend to a purée with the lemon juice and 1 tablespoon water.

Peel and chop the onion finely. Heat the butter in a saucepan and fry the onion for about 5 minutes until transparent. Add the flour and curry powder and cook uncovered for 3 minutes over gentle heat. Stir in the banana purée. Add the stock and bring to the boil. Simmer uncovered for 10 minutes. Season and simmer for 5 minutes more. Stir in the double cream and chopped coriander and serve hot.

POACHED EGGS ON A BED OF TOMATO WITH A LEEK SAUCE

Serves Four

Many elements from Jupiter's preferred ingredients are here: tomatoes, nutmeg and leek being the chief of them.

For the leek sauce
3 young leeks
1 pint/600ml water
3 oz/75g butter
salt and pepper
3 fl oz/85ml double cream
lemon juice

For the tomatoes
1 large onion
1 clove garlic
3 medium sticks celery
8 tomatoes
3 tablespoons olive oil
¼ teaspoon nutmeg
1 teaspoon tomato purée
salt and black pepper

For the eggs
1 tablespoon vinegar
4 large fresh eggs
chervil to decorate

Trim and wash the leeks very well. Separate the green from the white parts. Put the greens in a pan with the water and bring to the boil. Cook, uncovered, for at least 30 minutes, reducing the liquid to 6 fluid ounces/175ml. Strain and reserve the stock.

Cut the white part of the leeks into slices. Heat 2 ounces/50g of the butter in a saucepan and cook the leeks, covered, for about 8 minutes, until really tender. Put in the blender with the leek stock and blend to a purée. Put through a fine sieve and season. Put the leek purée back in the pan and stir in the double cream. Simmer briefly. Cut the remaining butter into pieces and whisk it in. Check the seasoning, adding lemon juice if necessary, and keep hot.

Peel and cut the onion in ¼ inch/5mm dice; peel and chop the garlic; wash and string the celery (if necessary) and cut into dice like the onion; peel, seed and dice the tomatoes.

Heat the oil in a saucepan over medium heat and fry the onion, garlic and celery for about 5 minutes without colouring. Add the nutmeg and fry a little longer. Add the tomatoes, tomato purée, salt and pepper. Cook gently, uncovered, until the liquid from the tomatoes has evaporated. Keep hot while you cook the eggs.

Bring a wide pan of water to the boil. Add the vinegar. Turn the heat down so that the water is barely moving. Break the eggs into cups and gently slide them into the water. If the water boils too fast, the eggs will be scrappy. Poach for about 5 minutes, so that the yolks are still runny.

While the eggs are poaching, divide the tomato and celery mixture between 4 hot plates. Remove the eggs with a slotted spoon, trim any ragged white and drain them well on kitchen paper. Place them on top of the tomato and celery mixture. Spoon the hot sauce over the eggs. Decorate with chervil leaves and serve.

SQUAB STUFFED WITH APRICOTS
Serves Four

The squab or young pigeon is a luxury item, fitting for Jupiter. Squab are not easy to come by, and wood pigeons are no substitute for this recipe — much too tough and dry. You could use quail or poussin, though the taste would be lighter. You need stock for this recipe so it would be sensible to trim the birds and make a pigeon stock (reserve the livers). Serve some parsnips or turnips to keep within Jupiter and a dish of fresh peas.

For the stuffing

3 oz/75g dried apricots
2 oz/50g raisins
½ onion
1 oz/25g butter
1 tablespoon pine kernels
3-4 oz/75-125g soft breadcrumbs
2 teaspoons chopped parsley
4 fl oz/120ml chicken or pigeon stock
salt and black pepper

For the squab

4 small squab, each about 12-16 oz/350-450g,
    prepared for roasting
salt and black pepper
1 fl oz/25ml olive oil
2 fl oz/50ml brandy
6 fl oz/175ml white wine
6 fl oz/175ml chicken or pigeon stock
1 teaspoon redcurrant jelly

For the croûtons

3 oz/75g butter
4 small pieces white bread, 3 inches/7.5cm square
squab livers, free of all gall
salt and black pepper
2 tablespoons double cream
1 teaspoon chopped parsley

Soak the apricots overnight, drain and chop; plump the raisins in warm water for 30 minutes, drain and chop; peel and chop the onion. Heat the butter in a pan and fry the onion gently for 5 minutes until transparent. Add the apricots, raisins and the rest of the ingredients. Mix well.

Rub the outside of the squab with salt and pepper and oil. Stuff with the apricot mixture. Secure front and back apertures with thread or cocktail sticks to stop the stuffing spilling. Put the birds in a heavy roasting pan and roast in a preheated oven at 425°F/220°C/Gas Mark 7 for 20 to 25 minutes. Although squab should not be overcooked, they should not be served rare either. To test pierce one of the legs with a skewer, if the juices that run out are clear the bird is done.

Drain any fat from the roasting pan and put the pan over heat. Warm the brandy, set it alight and pour over the birds. When the flames die down lift out the squab and keep warm.

Pour the wine into the pan and bubble up for 1 minute. Add the stock and boil to reduce by half. Add the redcurrant jelly and stir until dissolved. Taste for seasoning.

While the squab are roasting, prepare the croûtons. Heat the butter in a frying pan and fry the bread until brown on both sides. Lift out and reserve. Season the livers and fry them quickly in the same butter for about 1 minute, browning both sides but still pink in the centre. Press the livers through a fine sieve with the double cream. Mix in the chopped parsley. Spread on the croûtons. Warm gently in the oven when you are ready to serve.

Serve the squab whole on the liver croûtons, with the sauce poured round. Make sure everyone at the table has a sharp knife, otherwise, carve the birds yourself, removing the meat in four joints — legs and breasts — as quickly as possible.

GLAZED TURNIPS
Serves Four to Six

One of Jupiter's vegetables. It goes well with game, or as a vegetable course on its own with good bread. If you are lucky in your supplier, you will be able to get very, very young turnips so tender they need no peeling. On the presumption, however, that your supplies will be mixed, I have suggested a way of dealing with various sizes of root — still young mark you, old turnips would not be so satisfactory.

2 lb/900g young turnips
2 oz/50g butter
1 teaspoon sugar
4 fl oz/120ml port
4 fl oz/120ml chicken stock
salt

2 teaspoons wine vinegar
1 teaspoon crushed green peppercorns

Peel the turnips. Cut them in quarters and using a small sharp knife, turn them to even shapes about the size of a large clove of garlic.

Melt the butter in a heavy saucepan and stew the turnips, covered, for 5 minutes. Shake them periodically so that they are evenly coated with the butter. Add the sugar and continue to cook, covered, but shaking the pan, for 3 minutes. Turn the heat up and add the port. Bubble fiercely for

Strawberry Tart

20 seconds then add the stock and salt. Simmer, uncovered, over medium heat for about 10 minutes, occasionally shaking the pan. The liquid should evaporate slowly, leaving an intense syrup as the turnips are cooked tender. If it evaporates too quickly, add a little water; if too slowly, turn the heat up at the end. When reduced to 6 tablespoons of liquid, add the vinegar and peppercorns. Bubble fiercely and serve.

JASMINE CREAM WITH A MINT JELLY
Serves Four

Jupiter is the planet for teas, especially fragrant ones, although they are but occasional ingredients in recipes. Here, the flowery jasmine tea, very mild in flavour, is used to make a set cream.

For the tea cream
15 fl oz/450ml milk
½ oz/15g jasmine tea
3 egg yolks
1 oz/25g sugar
½ oz/15g powdered gelatine
1 tablespoon lemon juice mixed with 2 tablespoons cold water
3 fl oz/85ml double cream

For the mint jelly
10 leaves ginger or eau de cologne mint
1 teaspoon sugar
4 fl oz/120ml water
1 teaspoon powdered gelatine
1 tablespoon lemon juice mixed with 2 tablespoons old water
green food colouring

Scald the milk with the tea in an open pan. Infuse for about 5 minutes until it is the correct strength. Strain then put back on the heat. In a bowl, beat the egg yolks with the sugar until pale. Pour on the near boiling milk, stirring. Put the bowl over a pan of hot water on a low heat and cook the custard for about 10 minutes or until it coats the back of a spoon. Set it aside to cool.

Sprinkle the gelatine on the lemon juice and water to soften. Heat to dissolve, add to the custard and cool.

Whip the cream until firm and fold into the custard. Pour into a serving bowl and cool completely. Then put in the refrigerator to set.

Heat the mint leaves and the sugar in the water. When the sugar has dissolved, bring to just under boiling point. Take the pan off the heat and leave to infuse for 10 minutes. Strain.

Sprinkle the gelatine on the lemon juice and water to soften, then heat to dissolve. Add to the mint infusion. Add drops of colouring for the desired lurid shade of green. When cool but not set, pour carefully across the smooth top of the custard to form a very thin layer. Put the bowl in the refrigerator for the jelly to set.

STRAWBERRY TART
Serves Four

Jupiter has an enviable palette of fruit. This strawberry tart recipe figures in a Victorian book with the note 'good' appended: it is that and, for a bonus, it is simple and fast.

butter for the pie plate
12 oz/350g sweet shortcrust pastry
1 lb/450g strawberries
2 tablespoons kirsch
2 oz/50g caster sugar
4 eggs
icing sugar

Butter a 10 inch/25cm shallow pie plate, about 1 inch/2.5cm deep.

Roll out the pastry and line the pie plate. Prick the bottom all over with a fork. Rest in the refrigerator for 20 minutes. Cover the bottom with aluminium foil or greaseproof paper and fill with dried beans or rice. Bake in a preheated oven at 400°F/200°C/Gas Mark 6 for 15 to 20 minutes until a pale gold.

Wipe and hull the strawberries. Mash roughly and mix with the kirsch and sugar. Beat the eggs well and mix them thoroughly into the strawberries. Taste and add more sugar if necessary. Pour into the pastry case and bake at the same temperature as for the pastry for about 12 to 15 minutes until set. Dust with icing sugar.

SATURN

RULER OF CAPRICORN AND AQUARIUS

SATURN is the planet of discipline, hard work, austerity, tradition and simplicity. It is the ruler of old age and as Chronos is the Lord of Time. It judges articles and human qualities according to how useful they are, and has little time for luxury.

SATURN ENVIRONMENTS
These are simple and austere, though not unpleasant. They include places that cater for workers, and hence works canteens and, by contrast, old traditional coaching inns or hotels. The Saturn kitchen is unmodernized and specific items ruled by this planet include sinks, drains and refrigerators.

SATURN COOKING
Cooking methods are dry, and include baking, grilling or toasting. Food which requires cooking for a long time is also Saturnine. However, as it is the coldest of all the planets, it rules uncooked and crunchy food, such as raw carrots as well as iced foods.

SATURN FOODS
Plain and traditional, Saturn foods are dry rather than moist, healthy rather than rich. The health food movement is directed by this planet, as is the modern obsession with dieting and small portions. Saturnine tastes are typically sour, bitter, sharp and astringent. Food which is mouldy, such as blue cheese or high, such as well-hung game, is also ruled by this planet.

SATURN MEAT, FISH AND POULTRY
These include pork, bacon, ham and all shellfish (which are jointly ruled with the Moon). Saturn rules bones and substances made from them, such as gelatine.

SATURN VEGETABLES, GRAINS, ETC
Parsnips, spinach, onions, beetroot, potato, barley and lentils.

SATURN FRUIT AND NUTS
Quince, sloes, fruits which have a disagreeable smell such as durian, the Thai national fruit which is banned from enclosed public places, and anything with a shell is ruled by Saturn, including most nuts.

SATURN HERBS, SPICES AND FLAVOURINGS, ETC
Sage, capers, rue and vervain.

PARCELS OF CRAB IN SPINACH LEAVES
Serves Four

Beginning Saturn as we should continue: shellfish and an emphasis on the sour. Balsamic vinegar is an Italian speciality available at good delicatessens.

1 lb/450g picked white crab meat
grated zest of 1 lemon
¼ teaspoon cayenne pepper
salt
2 egg whites
20 large spinach leaves
3 tablespoons chopped fresh ginger root
For the salad
6 inch/15cm length *daikon* — white radish
2 carrots
1 teaspoon salt
2 teaspoons balsamic vinegar

First make the accompanying salad. Peel and trim the vegetables and cut them into fine matchsticks. Mix them in a bowl with the salt and leave for 5 minutes. Knead them between the fingers for 1 minute then squeeze hard to rid them of their waters then rinse well. In a clean bowl, toss them in the vinegar.

Mix the crab meat with the lemon zest, cayenne, salt and egg whites. Wash the spinach leaves thoroughly and blanch them for 20 seconds in a large pan of boiling salted water. Drain and dry. Remove their ribs. Make little parcels of crab with the spinach leaves as wrapping. Put them on a heatproof plate and cover closely with clingfilm. Put the plate on a rack. Put the rack in a pan or wok over boiling water, cover and steam them for 4 to 6 minutes.

Take out the parcels and put them on a serving dish. Put the ginger in a garlic press and express the juice over the crab parcels. Serve with the salad.

STIR FRIED PORK WITH CUMIN AND SPINACH
Serves Four

Pork, cumin, spinach: all Saturn's foods — in one pan. This is most easily cooked in a wok, but a large sauté pan will do. Serve with rice.

For the spinach
1½ lb/700g spinach
salt
4 tablespoons vegetable oil
1 clove garlic
½ teaspoon ground cumin
For the pork
1 lb/450g pork tenderloin
1 teaspoon chopped fresh ginger root
2 teaspoons cornflour
½ teaspoon salt
6 spring onions
2 tablespoons vegetable oil
2 tablespoons medium sherry
2 teaspoons soy sauce
1 teaspoon sugar
cayenne pepper

Wash the spinach and strip its larger stalks. Put in a large pan of boiling water with salt and 1 tablespoon of the oil. Blanch for 1 minute. Drain and refresh under cold running water.

Peel and chop the garlic finely. Heat the remaining oil and cook the garlic and cumin gently for 1 minute. Add the spinach and continue to cook, over slightly higher heat, for 2 minutes. Keep warm while you cook the pork.

Trim the pork well and cut into thin pieces. Put in a bowl with the ginger, cornflour and salt. Rub with your fingers to coat the pork well. Trim and chop the spring onions.

In the same pan you used for the spinach, add the oil, and fry the pork and onion over gentle to medium heat. Cook for 2 minutes, stirring and tossing. Add the sherry, soy sauce, sugar and cayenne. Turn the heat up and fry for 1 minute longer. Place the spinach on a serving dish, pile the pork in the centre and serve.

SALAD OF SALSIFY WITH A RED DRESSING
Serves Four

If salsify (or scorzonera — similar to eat) is not a Saturn vegetable, it should be. Dull in colour, muted though distinctive in taste, it conforms to many of Saturn's requirements. This recipe is for a salad, lifted to the lurid tones that are enjoyed by Aquarians (who interpret Saturn in a fauvist mode) by the vivid hue of the beetroot vinaigrette — now, beetroot *is* a Saturnine root. There are a number of beetroot salads, with dandelion, chicory or celery that are worth exploring for other Saturnine repasts. The effect of this salad is spoiled if the salsify lose their whiteness. Therefore I have suggested a small plain dressing in the first instance, before surrounding the vegetable with a sea of carmine. Remember that the salsify discolours in contact with the air before cooking. This is the reason for using a *blanc* in which to boil it. Like

the white heads of chicory, most salsify and scorzonera are imported from Belgium.

2 tablespoons flour
2 pints/1.1 litres water
1 lemon
salt
1 tablespoon oil
12 salsify

For the plain vinaigrette

2 teaspoons wine vinegar
1 teaspoon chopped tarragon
3 tablespoons olive oil
salt and white pepper

Salad of Salsify with a Red Dressing

For the beetroot vinaigrette
1 ready-cooked beetroot
1 tablespoon wine vinegar
½ teaspoon English mustard powder
6 tablespoons oil
salt and white pepper

To prepare the *blanc*, whisk the flour into the cold water. Squeeze the lemon and add the juice and the squeezed out lemon shells. Season with salt and add the oil. Scrub and trim the salsify. Peel with a swivel peeler and cut each root into 1 inch/2.5cm lengths as you prepare it. Put them straight into the *blanc*. Bring to the boil and cook gently, uncovered, for 30 minutes until tender.

Meanwhile, prepare the plain vinaigrette. Put the vinegar into a small bowl and whisk in the tarragon, oil and seasoning.

Drain and rinse the salsify under a cool tap, dry in a cloth and dress immediately in the plain vinaigrette.

The beetroot vinaigrette is coloured by cutting the beetroot (bought cooked and peeled) into cubes and putting in a blender with the vinegar. Blend to a purée and strain the juice through a fine sieve into a bowl. Whisk in the mustard and oil, adding the oil very slowly indeed to maintain the emulsion. Season. Pile the salsify in the middle of plates and pour the beetroot vinaigrette around it.

CHICORY WITH MUSTARD
Serves Four
8 small heads Witloof chicory
juice of ½ lemon
salt
2 oz/50g butter

For the sauce
2 egg yolks
lemon juice
2 oz/50g butter, cut in pieces
1 teaspoon English mustard powder

First make the sauce. Put the egg yolks in a bowl with a squeeze of lemon and 2 teaspoons cold water. Set the bowl over a pan of hot water and whisk until creamy adding the butter piece by

piece. Do not allow to overheat or the emulsion will be lost. Stir in the mustard powder. Keep warm while you cook the chicory.

Trim the chicory. Put it with the lemon juice and salt in a pan of boiling water. Cover and cook for about 10 to 15 minutes or until just tender. To test if done, poke the base of the chicory with a skewer. Drain very well.

Melt the butter in a pan that will hold the chicory in a single layer. Put in the chicory and cook over a medium heat for about 5 minutes, turning them in the butter until golden brown.

Turn the chicory out onto a serving dish, pour the sauce over them and serve immediately.

A LAYERED CITRUS SOUFFLE
Serves Six
Saturn claims no citrus fruits to itself, but their tartness should be justification enough for their inclusion. The recipe given here is the more Saturnine for its use of gelatine for setting, for the pale colours of the composition and for its austerity inasmuch as there are only whites, no yolks, of egg in the soufflés. (A mayonnaise or hollandaise sauce will be a good way of using the yolks!) The method given below is repetitious, for there are three soufflés in one, all following largely the same method. You will need a large 2½ pint/1.4 litre soufflé dish or mould. Oil it with a neutral oil (or almond oil) if you want to turn the soufflé out. Put all the cream and the egg whites in the refrigerator to chill before you start.

For the jelly
1 small jar about 8 oz/225g redcurrant jelly
juice of 1 lemon

For the lime soufflé
2 limes
3 oz/75g sugar
1 teaspoon powdered gelatine
7 fl oz/200ml double cream
2 egg whites

For the lemon soufflé
2 lemons
3 oz/75g sugar
1 teaspoon powdered gelatine

7 fl oz/200ml double cream
2 egg whites

For the grapefruit soufflé
1 grapefruit
2 oz/50g sugar
1 teaspoon powdered gelatine
7 fl oz/200ml double cream
2 egg whites

Melt the redcurrant jelly with the lemon juice over a very gentle heat. Keep cool, but do not allow it to set.

Grate the zest off the limes and squeeze out their juice. Put the juice and zest into a small saucepan with the sugar and sprinkle the gelatine on top. Soften, then dissolve by gentle heating and stirring. Pour into a large bowl and cool. Whip the double cream to a soft firmness and fold into the citrus mixture as it is on the point of setting. Put in the refrigerator. Whisk the egg whites to stiff peaks and fold them into the cream, again as it is on the point of setting. Put carefully into the oiled mould, trying to get as smooth a top surface as possible. Float a layer of half the redcurrant jelly over the top. Leave in the refrigerator to set.

Proceed with the lemons as you did with the limes. Put the completed soufflé mixture on top of the layer of redcurrant jelly. Again, keep the top as smooth as possible and float the rest of the redcurrant jelly over it. Leave once more in the refrigerator.

Make the final soufflé, this time with the grapefruit proceeding in the same way as before. Put that on the top and, if you are going to turn it out for serving, make the top as smooth as you can. Chill before serving.

COFFEE GRANITA
Serves Four
The bitterness of coffee makes it a natural subject of Saturn. Here, it is broadened by the addition of caramel and perfumed by a little cardamom.
4 oz/125g coffee, finely ground
seeds from 2 cardamom pods
4 oz/125g sugar

1 pint/600ml water
sweet biscuits for serving

Put the coffee, cardamom and half the sugar in a pan with the water. Bring nearly to the boil, take off the heat and infuse for 20 minutes, then strain.

Put the rest of the sugar in a pan and heat to a strong caramel. Just before it starts to burn, stop it by gingerly adding the coffee (take care, it will hiss and spit). Stir to dissolve the caramel. Set aside to cool.

Put the mixture into a tray or a container and leave in the freezer without disturbing it. Serve as shavings in glasses, with sweet biscuits.

BROWN SUGAR MERINGUES WITH COFFEE BRANDY CREAM
Serves Six
This is the most indulgent of desserts but the use of coffee is justification for its inclusion here.

For the meringues
4 egg whites
4 oz/125g caster sugar
4 oz/125g raw cane sugar

For the coffee brandy cream
10 fl oz/300ml double cream
1 tablespoon instant coffee
2 teaspoons caster sugar
2 tablespoons brandy
2 oz/50g bitter chocolate for grating

Line 2 baking trays with silicone paper.

In a clean grease-free bowl, whisk the egg whites to soft peaks. Add the sugar, a tablespoon at a time, and continue to whisk until really stiff. Using a star shaped nozzle, pipe the meringue onto the trays in basket shapes. Bake in a preheated oven at 275°F/140°C/Gas Mark 1 for about 1 hour, until the colour has changed slightly. Turn off the heat and leave the meringues to dry in the residual heat of the oven until cool. There will be at least 12 baskets; to preserve store them in an airtight container.

Whip the cream together with the coffee, sugar and brandy to a firm consistency. Fill the baskets and serve with chocolate grated over the top.

FOOD FOR LOVE

The association between astrology and aphrodisiacs is enshrined in the fact that every year on St Valentine's Day, the feast day of lovers, the Sun is in Aquarius, the sign of the gourmet.

The fascinating connections between the planets and specific aphrodisiacs are firmly rooted in the ancient doctrine of signatures, on the basis of which all items of food were assigned to particular planets whose characteristics they were said to share. Accordingly all phallic shaped items were assigned to Mars, the planet of male sexuality, while soft and fleshy foods reminiscent of the female organs were placed under the rulership of Venus, the goddess of the female sex. This explains why in the East rhino horns are thought to be a male stimulant, and ground deer antlers mixed with tea are popular for the same reason. Oysters, ruled by the Moon, the other female planet, are also thought to possess powerful aphrodisiac properties. Casanova is reputed to have eaten fifty oysters every evening as a prelude to his nocturnal activities. Recently a dish of oysters with cardamom and crushed coriander — ruled by Venus — was recommended as a suitable appetizer for a romantic evening.

Other astrological aphrodisiacs include asparagus, beans and, less appealing, the brains of doves, all of which are ruled by Venus. The most celebrated Martian stimulants are basil, capers and, most legendary of all, chocolate, a substance with many amorous associations. Casanova, who filled chocolates with Spanish fly, drank it instead of champagne, while Madame du Barry, mistress of Louis XV of France, gave chocolate to all her lovers.

According to the sixteenth century scholar, Henry Cornelius Agrippa, walnuts and chestnuts, ruled by Venus, were originally thought to stimulate lust because they caused flatulence, a logic which probably also underlies the theory that beans, also ruled by Venus, stimulate sexual desire.

In some cases modern science has discovered chemical explanations for traditional superstition: Spanish fly, for example, long used to stimulate male livestock into breeding, has been found to contain a urogenital stimulant known as cantharides. In West Africa, the bark of the yohimbe tree boiled in water and drunk as an aphrodisiac, has been found to contain another stimulant, yohimbine. A West Indian recipe mixes yohimbe bark with puréed peppercorns, chillis, pimentos — all ruled by Mars — and aubergines and vanilla. Unfortunately, both cantharides and yohimbine are toxic, cantharides causing the traditional Martian ailments of blisters and burns.

Other aphrodisiacs are safer. When Madame Pompadour served her lovers with celery soup, she was unaware that when heated it is thought to release a substance similar to pheromone, a chemical substance secreted externally by certain animals to attract the opposite sex. Bananas, whose phallic shape associates them with Mars, contain a mildly hallucinogenic alkaloid. Unfortunately, the vast amount you would need to eat before entering a state of romantic dreams precludes this short cut to an amorous situation.

Ultimately, all good food has an aphrodisiac effect if it lessens stress and strain, which is responsible for reducing the libido, and heightens sensual awareness. Pay attention to aroma, colour, texture, shape and presentation of the meal, and, if possible, get someone else to cook it for you. Slaving in a hot kitchen is the last thing likely to induce an amorous mood. Venus also offers the advice that atmosphere is important, and the psychological effect of a well prepared meal, soft music and subdued lighting creates exactly the right conditions for a successful seduction.

OYSTERS POACHED WITH A JULIENNE OF VEGETABLES AND CHAMPAGNE

Serves two

1 carrot
1 leek
2 sticks celery
16 fresh oysters, as large as you can afford
approx. 5 fl oz/150ml champagne or sparkling
  dry white wine
1 tablespoon double cream
1 oz/25g butter
salt and pepper

Wash and prepare the vegetables, cut them into thin matchsticks — as thin as you can make them. Cook them in a steamer for a very short time — a minute or two. Keep hot.

Open the oysters and strain their juices into a small pan. Reserve the oysters. Add to the juices an equivalent amount of champagne. Boil and reduce by three-quarters. Finish the sauce by stirring in the cream and whisking in the butter. Season, then add the oysters for just as long as it takes to heat them through. They do not need to be 'cooked' otherwise they will shrivel.

Arrange the vegetables on plates, lift out the oysters and put them on top and pour the sauce over them.

ROAST MONKFISH WITH BLACK PEPPER AND PORT

Serves Two

1 lb/450g monkfish tail
½ small onion
2 oz/50g butter
flour seasoned with salt
1 tablespoon black peppercorns
4 fl oz/120ml port
7 fl oz/200ml double cream
lemon juice

Use the monkfish on the bone. Get the fishmonger to skin it and to lift the inner membrane, which causes it to contract during cooking.

Chop the onion. Heat the butter in a roasting pan. Add the onion and cook gently until soft. Dredge the fish with seasoned flour. Crush the black pepper with the back of a spoon and roll the fish in it. Place the fish on top of the onion and roast it in a preheated hot oven at 425°F/220°C/Gas Mark 7, basting frequently, for 40 to 45 minutes or until tender. Test by seeing how freely the flesh comes away from the bone with a knife tip. Lift out the fish, place on a heated dish and keep warm.

Put the roasting pan on top of the stove. Pour in the port and bring to the boil. Continue boiling until the sauce is reduced and syrupy. Stir in the cream and boil until thick and smooth. Adjust the seasoning, adding a little lemon juice if necessary. Strain the sauce around the fish and serve.

FILLET OF BEEF WITH DOUBLE MUSHROOM SAUCE

Serves Two

2 fillet steaks, each about 6 oz/175g
salt and pepper
1 tablespoon oil
½ oz/15g butter

Sauce

1 packet (approx ½ oz/15g) dried boletus
  mushrooms
1 large onion
12 oz/350g mushrooms
8 fl oz/250ml red wine
1 vegetable bouillon cube
4 oz/125g butter
1 tablespoon redcurrant jelly
salt and pepper

First make the sauce. Put the dried mushrooms in a small bowl, cover with cold water and leave to soak for 1 to 2 hours.

Meanwhile, peel and chop the onion; chop the fresh mushrooms. Put the onion and red wine in a pan and bring to the boil. Add the bouillon cube and chopped fresh mushrooms and continue to boil until there is only 1 tablespoon of liquid left in the pan. Tip the contents of the pan into a blender and process until puréed.

Drain the soaking mushrooms and chop roughly. Reserve the soaking water. Heat 1 ounce/25g of the butter in a frying pan and fry the mushrooms for 1 to 2 minutes. Remove the mushrooms. Add the reserved soaking water to the frying pan and, stirring and scraping, boil fiercely to reduce. Return the dried mushroom to the pan along with the fresh mushroom purée and continue to cook. Stir in the redcurrant jelly and salt and pepper to taste. Whisk in the remaining butter, a little at a time.

Just before the sauce is ready, season the steaks and fry in a mixture of butter and oil. Serve immediately with the sauce.

PASSION FRUIT SOUFFLE
Serves Two
butter for the dish
1 egg yolk
2½ oz/65g caster sugar plus extra for the sauce
2 egg whites
4 fl oz/120ml passion fruit pulp
juice of ¼ orange

Butter a small soufflé dish.

In a bowl, beat the egg yolk and half the sugar until pale yellow. In another bowl, beat the egg whites, adding the rest of the sugar, bit by bit, until they form high peaks. Add 3 tablespoons of the passion fruit to the yolks and mix well. Fold in the egg whites carefully.

Pour the mixture into the soufflé dish and bake in a preheated oven at 425°F/220°C/Gas Mark 7 for about 10 minutes.

Meanwhile, heat the rest of the passion fruit pulp with the orange juice. Stir in sugar to taste and serve as a sauce for the soufflé.

STRAWBERRIES WITH BLACK PEPPER AND ORANGE SORBET
Serves Two
8 oz/225g fresh strawberries
1 oz/25g caster sugar
black pepper
mint leaves for decoration

Sorbet
3 oranges
5 fl oz/150ml water
juice of ½ lemon
6 oz/175g caster sugar
1 egg white

To make the sorbet, peel the zest of the oranges and squeeze the juice. Put the zest and the water in a small pan and bring to the boil. Remove from the heat and leave to infuse for 20 minutes.

Strain the water into the orange juice. Add the lemon juice and sugar, stir to dissolve and leave to cool. When quite cold pour into a container, cover and put in the freezer.

After about 2 hours, when the mixture is just beginning to set, remove it from the freezer and tip out into a bowl. Whisk the egg white until it forms firm peaks, then beat it into the sorbet. Return the mixture to the freezer for at least 4 hours before serving.

Meanwhile, hull the strawberries and cut them in half lengthwise. Sprinkle with the sugar and leave for 1 hour.

To serve, scoop out the sorbet onto a chilled dish and surround with the strawberries. Grind black pepper over the strawberries and decorate with mint leaves.

PISTACHIO CREAM
Serves two
4 oz/125g unsalted shelled pistachio nuts
½ tablespoon brandy
½ pint/300ml double cream
2 egg yolks

Put the pistachio nuts in a bowl. Pour in enough boiling water to cover. Leave for 2 to 3 minutes then remove the nuts and rub off the skins. Purée the nuts in a blender with the brandy. Put the cream in a saucepan or double boiler. Beat the egg yolks and stir into the cream along with the pistachio purée. Stir constantly over gentle heat until the custard has thickened. Do not allow to boil or the custard will curdle.

FOOD FOR PROFIT

Food is clearly an important psychological component of all social gatherings, including business meetings. As the oldest psychological system in the world, astrology inevitably has something to say on the subject.

The first consideration is whether the other people involved are allies or rivals. Have you already settled a deal and formed a partnership, or do you wish to persuade your rivals to support you, or do you intend to take them over?

When dealing with rivals you should probably take note of the ancient astrological rules for seizing an enemy castle. Unfortunately, like the barons of old, you would need your own private astrologer to advise on the minute by minute fluctuations of the celestial influences to succeed in such an enterprise. It is probably easier to take your colleagues' or rivals' birth signs into account within the general astrological rules relating to business.

In astrological terms wealth is ruled by Jupiter and hard work by Saturn, so the ideal business meal should be a balance between the two. Incline to Jupiter if you wish to impress: serve lavish roasts — lamb, venison, chicken or pheasant — with rich sauces, accompanied by fine wines and generous desserts.

Yet, if there is work to be done, without doubt Saturn is the better bet. If you need to convince your colleagues that you can handle their commission, work to a high standard and deliver the goods on time, relatively simply cooked food will serve your cause. Pork, ham, bacon, crab, lobster or other shellfish provide an ideal Saturnine main course. The desserts should be healthy, to demonstrate that you will complete the job without a heart attack. Fruit suits the Saturnine temperament, and a simple fresh fruit salad will be appreciated.

The other planets, however, may all have a role to play, too. Mars, which rules stimulants, can aid the concentration. Tea with the meal, if an oriental dish is chosen, helps focus the thoughts, and coffee with chocolates, especially mint chocolates, prevents after-lunch depression.

Venus, which stimulates social intercourse, assists in the conclusion of amicable agreements, and rules similar foods to Jupiter. It may help to conclude the meal with rather more lavish fruits than Saturn would normally permit. Large juicy peaches or mangoes, for example, could form the basis of a Venusian fruit salad.

If you want to show you care, look to the Moon (which, like Saturn, rules shellfish), and serve melon or a similar watery fruit.

On the other hand, if clear communication and a grasp of detail is necessary, look to Mercury, and 'brain food'. The food considered best for the brain is fish, which is ruled by the Moon. All things considered crab or lobster is the most suitable choice as long as you do not serve it to someone with whom you wish to forge a long-term partnership. Symbolically a creature inside a hard shell does not bode well for a close relationship.

Remember, too, that all the planets rule mood and atmosphere, hence your Saturnine meal should be presented in a sober and traditional setting. If at a restaurant, the ambience for a working lunch should be plain, almost austere, and free from any hint of opulence. The Jupiterian lunch, on the other hand, may quite happily take place in lavish surroundings where no expense has been spared.

SCRAMBLED EGGS WITH SAFFRON
Serves Four

The spotlight is on the eggs, with a touch of Leo in the saffron. Eggs are ruled by Venus and the Moon, aspects therefore of sociability and amicable agreement as well as a sharp brain.

4 slices bread, crusts removed
½ oz/15g butter plus extra for frying bread
1 packet (125mg) saffron, in stamen or powder
3 tablespoons strong beef or chicken stock
8 eggs
4 tablespoons single cream
salt and black pepper

Fry the bread in butter and keep warm. Put the saffron, stock and butter into the pan which you will use for the eggs and cook for a few seconds to bring out the flavour of the spice. Beat the eggs, then beat in the cream and seasoning. Add them to the saffron. Scramble over a very low heat, stirring all the while, until they are just setting yet are still quite creamy. Serve on the fried bread.

PHEASANT SAUSAGES
Serves Four

As a counterweight to Saturn, this is a wholly Jupiter affair of rich little sausages filled with game. They need to be accompanied by something sharp: an apple sauce or some red cabbage cooked with apple. This amount should be enough for an 18 inch/45cm length of sausage casing, to be bought from the butcher.

1 oz/25g soft white breadcrumbs
4 tablespoons milk
2 shallots
½ oz/15g butter
4 oz/125g pheasant flesh, uncooked, off the bone and skinned
2 oz/50g fat salt pork belly
2 oz/50g lean pork
1 egg
2 juniper berries
salt and black pepper
sausage casing
oil and butter for frying the sausages, if needed

Soak the breadcrumbs in the milk. Chop the shallots finely. Heat the butter in a small pan and fry the shallots gently for about 3 minutes, without colouring. Set aside to cool.

Chop the meats very finely indeed but not to a paste — there should be some texture to the sausages. Beat the egg, crush the juniper berries and combine all ingredients. Season highly with salt and especially black pepper.

Fill the sausage casing, using a piping bag. Twist and tie into short lengths and cut into sausages. Cook them in barely simmering water for about 8 minutes. Drain and dry. If you wish to serve them immediately, they may be offered boiled, or they may be grilled or fried in butter and oil to give them colour.

LOBSTER IN A TOP HAT
Serves Four

If Jupiter is the lavish planet, and Saturn that of hard work, the combination is well met in this dish of lobster with a fish soufflé topping. It needs little accompaniment beyond some plain rice and a green salad. One small nod to economy is that this dish will need less lobster per person than a plain lobster mayonnaise or other boiled lobster dish.

1 lobster, about 2 lb/900g
salt

For the topping
2 eggs
6 oz/175g cooked, boned white fish — haddock, plaice, sole or whiting
5 fl oz/150ml double cream
juice of ½ lemon
salt and pepper
nutmeg

For finishing
2 oz/50g butter
2 fl oz/50ml Sercial Madeira
3 fl oz/85ml double cream
black pepper
mace

Bring a large pan of heavily salted water to the boil. Drop the lobster in and cook, covered, for

20 minutes from the time it comes back to the boil. Place immediately under running cold water and cool. Split the lobster in half lengthwise and extract all the meat, disposing of the intestinal duct and the sac. Cut the tail flesh into collops. Reserve the white body and claw meat apart from the head cream.

Next prepare the topping. Separate the eggs. Pound or process the fish and mix with the lobster head cream. Put through a sieve into a bowl. Mix in the cream, lemon juice and egg yolks. Season with salt, pepper and nutmeg. Whisk the egg whites until stiff and fold them in.

To finish, melt the butter in a pan and warm the lobster flesh very gently for 2 minutes. Add the Madeira and boil for 10 seconds. Turn the heat down and add the cream. Season with pepper and mace. Divide between 4 gratin dishes and spoon the topping over. Bake in a preheated oven at 425°F/220°C/Gas Mark 7 for 10 minutes. Serve immediately.

BURST PIPES: LEEKS WITH PEPPERS, TOMATOES, GARLIC AND ANCHOVY
Serves Four
Leeks are one of Jupiter's vegetables, tomatoes are another. The addition of Martian capsicum and garlic, therefore, derogates but little from the Jupiter thrust of this dish, softened astrologically if not in taste by Lunar anchovies.
12 small leeks
salt
3 red peppers
5 cloves garlic
8 tomatoes
3 tablespoons olive oil
12 anchovy fillets
black pepper
2 oz/50g butter plus extra for the dish
2 oz/50g soft breadcrumbs
Trim and wash the leeks well, keeping only the whites and softer green parts. Boil in salted water for 10 to 15 minutes or until just tender. Drain well. Cut in half lengthwise. Grill or roast the red peppers until the skin has blistered all over. Rub off the skin, remove the seeds and stalks and chop finely; peel and chop the garlic; skin, seed and chop the tomatoes.

Heat the olive oil in a pan and fry the peppers and garlic over very gentle heat for 4 minutes. Add the tomatoes and continue to cook, uncovered, for about 5 minutes or until the tomato dries up a little. Season with black pepper.

Grease a gratin dish and place a layer of half the leeks in the bottom. Spread over the tomato and garlic mixture. Top with the anchovy fillets followed by the remaining leeks. Spread breadcrumbs on top, dot with butter and bake in the top of a preheated oven at 400°F/200°C/Gas Mark 6 for about 15 minutes or until browned.

TROPICAL DIPLOMAT PUDDING
Serves Four
Most puddings are more appropriate to Jupiter or Venus than to Saturn. If you need to emphasize that side of the meal, you will go without dessert altogether.
12 kiwi fruit
juice of 1 lemon
8 oz/225g strawberries
3 oz/75g sugar
oil for greasing the mould
24 sponge fingers
framboise, poire or kirsch eau-de-vie
cream for serving
Peel the kiwi and slice thinly. Squeeze the lemon juice over them. Wipe and hull the strawberries. Slice them and sprinkle with sugar.

Grease a 2 pint/1.1 litre bowl or mould. Lay a covering of sponge fingers across the bottom. Sprinkle them with a little liqueur. Cover this layer with one of kiwi fruit and their juice. Repeat a layer of sponge. Put in a layer of strawberries, and so on until all are used up. Finish with a layer of sponge. Place a saucer or plate inside the mould and weight it with a 2 pound/900g weight. Leave to consolidate in the refrigerator overnight. Turn out and eat with cream.

FOOD INDEX

This list has been compiled from traditional sources. Many foods combine the characters of more than one planet or sign of the Zodiac.

GENERAL

Berries	Venus, Virgo
Drinks	Moon, Aquarius, Pisces
Fish	Moon, Pisces
Flowers	Gemini, Libra, Aquarius
Fruit	Venus, Jupiter, Taurus, Aries, Leo, Sagittarius, Pisces, Moon
Grains	Mercury
Herbs	Mercury, Venus
Nuts	Sun
Poultry	Venus, Gemini, Libra, Sagittarius
Roots	Taurus, Virgo, Capricorn
Seeds	Aries, Leo, Sagittarius, Virgo
Shellfish	Moon, Saturn, Cancer
Spices, Hot	Mars
Water Birds	Cancer, Pisces, Aquarius

MEAT, FISH AND POULTRY

Bacon	Saturn
Beef	Moon, Venus, Taurus
Chicken	Moon, Venus, Jupiter, Gemini, Leo, Sun
Cockles	Cancer, Moon, Saturn
Cod	Pisces, Moon, Saturn
Crab	Cancer, Moon, Saturn
Dove	Venus, Jupiter
Duck	Gemini, Aquarius, Pisces, Moon
Frogs	Cancer, Scorpio, Moon
Goat	Sun, Venus, Mars, Aries, Capricorn
Goose	Gemini, Aquarius, Pisces, Moon
Haddock	Moon, Pisces
Ham	Moon, Saturn
Hare	Mercury
Lamb	Jupiter, Aries, Leo, Capricorn, Sun
Lobster	Cancer, Moon, Venus, Saturn
Mackerel	Pisces, Moon
Monkfish	Pisces, Moon
Mussels	Cancer, Moon, Saturn
Mullet	Moon, Mercury
Oysters	Cancer, Moon, Saturn
Partridge	Venus, Jupiter
Pheasant	Jupiter
Pike	Mars
Plaice	Pisces, Moon
Pork	Saturn

Prawns	Moon
Rabbit	Moon, Venus
Salmon	Pisces, Moon, Venus
Sardines	Pisces, Moon
Shark	Moon, Mars, Jupiter
Shrimps	Moon
Snails	Cancer, Scorpio, Saturn, Moon
Sole	Pisces, Moon
Squid	Pisces, Moon
Trout	Pisces, Moon
Tuna	Pisces, Moon, Jupiter
Turkey	Gemini
Veal	Venus
Venison	Venus, Jupiter, Aries, Mercury

DAIRY PRODUCTS

Butter	Taurus
Cheese	Taurus
Milk	Taurus
Yoghurt	Taurus

VEGETABLES, GRAINS, PULSES, ETC.

Artichoke	Venus, Pisces, Taurus
Asparagus	Venus, Jupiter
Aubergine	Mars
Barley	Sun, Moon, Jupiter, Saturn
Beans	Venus, Mercury
Beetroot	Saturn, Scorpio, Sagittarius
Buckwheat	Venus
Cabbage	Moon, Cancer, Pisces
Capsicum	Mars
Carrots	Mercury, Leo
Cauliflower	Moon
Celery	Mercury
Chickpeas	Jupiter
Chicory	Moon, Jupiter
Courgette	Moon
Cucumber	Moon
Dandelion	Venus
Endive	Capricorn, Jupiter, Moon
Fennel	Mercury, Virgo, Gemini
Kale	Moon
Gourds	Moon, Capricorn, Pisces
Leek	Mars, Jupiter
Lettuce	Moon
Lentils	Saturn
Maize	Sun
Marrow	Moon
Millet	Venus
Mushrooms	Moon
Nettles	Mars, Leo
Oats	Mercury
Onion	Moon, Mars, Saturn, Sagittarius
Parsnip	Venus, Saturn, Jupiter
Potato	Moon, Saturn

Pumpkin	Moon
Radish	Mars, Sagittarius
Rice	Sun, Jupiter, Cancer
Rye	Venus
Seaweed	Moon
Sorrel	Venus, Gemini, Virgo
Spinach	Saturn
Squash	Moon
Sugar Cane	Sun, Jupiter
Tomato	Moon, Jupiter
Turnip	Jupiter, Gemini, Cancer, Pisces
Watercress	Moon, Cancer
Wheat	Venus, Jupiter

FRUIT AND NUTS

Almond	Sun, Venus, Jupiter
Apples	Venus, Jupiter, Scorpio
Apricots	Jupiter, Venus
Barberry	Mars
Bilberry	Jupiter
Blackberry	Capricorn
Blackcurrants	Venus
Cherries	Venus
Cherries, Black	Capricorn
Chestnut	Jupiter
Currants	Venus, Jupiter
Coconut	Sun
Dates	Venus
Fig	Venus
Gooseberry	Venus
Grapes	Venus
Hazelnut	Mercury
Lemon	Sun
Mango	Venus
Melon	Moon
Mulberry	Mercury
Olive	Sun, Venus, Saturn
Orange	Sun, Venus, Jupiter
Peach	Venus
Pear	Venus
Pineapple	Mars
Plum	Venus
Pomegranate	Sun
Quince	Saturn
Raisins	Venus, Jupiter
Raspberry	Venus
Redcurrant	Venus
Rhubarb	Mars, Jupiter, Gemini
Sloe	Saturn, Virgo
Strawberry	Venus, Jupiter
Walnut	Sun, Venus, Mercury
Water Melon	Moon

HERBS, SPICES AND FLAVOURINGS

Aniseed	Jupiter, Gemini
Basil	Mars, Scorpio
Bay Leaf	Sun, Leo

Borage	Jupiter, Gemini	*Gelatine*	Saturn	*Poppy Seeds*	Moon
Camomile	Sun, Gemini, Libra	*Ginger*	Sun, Mars	*Rosemary*	Sun, Moon, Aries
Capers	Saturn, Mars, Aries	*Ginseng*	Jupiter	*Rue*	Saturn, Sun, Mars, Leo
Carob	Saturn	*Hops*	Mars	*Saffron*	Sun, Leo, Sagittarius,
Caraway Seed	Mercury	*Horseradish*	Mars		Taurus
Cayenne	Mars	*Hyssop*	Moon, Jupiter, Cancer,	*Sage*	Sun, Saturn, Jupiter,
Chervil	Jupiter		Gemini		Cancer
Chilli	Mars	*Jasmine*	Jupiter	*Salt*	Aquarius
Chives	Mars	*Liquorice*	Mercury	*Savory*	Mercury, Venus
Cinnamon	Sun, Jupiter, Aries	*Linden Flower*	Venus	*Sesame*	Jupiter
Cloves	Jupiter, Venus	*Lovage*	Sun, Sagittarius	*Spearmint*	Jupiter
Coffee	Mars, Saturn	*Mace*	Sun	*Sugar*	Sun, Jupiter, Cancer, Pisces
Comfrey	Saturn, Cancer,	*Maple Syrup*	Jupiter	*Sunflower Seeds*	Sun
	Sagittarius, Capricorn	*Marjoram*	Mercury, Aries	*Tamarind*	Mars
Coriander	Venus, Saturn	*Mint*	Jupiter, Venus, Aries, Leo	*Tea*	Mars
Cumin	Saturn, Aquarius	*Mustard*	Sun, Mars	*Thyme*	Venus, Jupiter, Aries, Leo
Dandelion	Venus	*Nutmeg*	Sun, Jupiter, Aries	*Treacle*	Mercury
Dill	Mercury	*Oregano*	Venus	*Turmeric*	Sagittarius
Fennel Seed	Mercury, Virgo	*Parsley*	Mercury, Venus	*Vervain*	Sun, Mercury, Saturn,
Fenugreek	Venus, Mercury	*Pepper*	Mars		Venus, Libra, Saggitarius
Garlic	Mars, Sagittarius	*Peppermint*	Sun, Venus, Jupiter	*Yarrow*	Venus

INDEX

Almond and cardamom pudding 91
Anchoiade — anchovy toast 14-15
Apple
  crumble with cinnamon 27
  fool with ginger 35
  flamed with Calvados 75
  poached Balkan style 91
Apricot toast 51
Artichoke
  fried Tuscan style 25-6
  tarts with soufflé topping 128
Asparagus
  gratin 82
  salad Japanese style 62
Aubergine
  caviar 54
  custard with coconut and
   cumin 54-5
  fried with green coriander
   sauce 90-1
  and parsnip chips 124
  puree with chilli 78
  sweet and sour 49-50
Avocado
  and cucumber salad 42
  mousse with three sauces 122

Banana curry soup 140
Barley cream 59
Beans
  with saffron, tomato and egg 74
  French, with hazelnuts 24
Beef
  fillet (Hungarian platter) 80-1
  fillet with double mushroom
   sauce 152-3

fillet with walnut and horseradish sauce 23
fillet/sirloin with mustard
  sauce 48
rump stuffed with salami and
  cheese 23-4
Biscuits, seed and spice 83
Bread
  onion ring 34-5
  Persian with cheese, herbs and
   salad 26
  San Francisco sourdough 33-4

Cabbage rolls, stuffed 97-8
Calf's liver with Dubonnet and
  orange 47
Camembert toast 106
Carrot
  and coriander soup 30
  and courgettes with mint
   sauce 112-113
  with cider sauce 106
  with dried fruit 57
Cauliflower
  deep fried 34
  Punjabi style 90
Celeriac remoulade 30-1
Cheesecake 82-3
Cherries with raspberry fool 136
Chestnut and chocolate cake 113
Chicken
  breast with cucumber 39-40
  Catalan 79-80
  and cucumber salad 62-3
  Savoyarde 63-4
  in shrimp and almond sauce

from Brazil 55-6
Tagine with apples 40-1
Tandoorised 111-2
with apple and horseradish 87-8
with peaches and cinnamon 24
Chicken liver toast with pine
  kernels and leaf salad 46
Cod with shrimp sauce 102
Coffee
  flan with chocolate sauce 137
  granita 149
Corn and marigold pudding 31-2
Couscous salad 105-06
Crab
  bisque 38
  claws with ginger 110
  parcels in spinach leaves 146
Crayfish, freshwater, with
  lemon sauce 94
Cream
  Atholl Brose 43
  burnt 19
  cheese with soft fruit 83
  hearts of 30-1
  little mocha 74-5
  pistachio 153
  Ricotta al caffe 59
Cucumber salad 73
Curry as in Bombay 47
Custard
  coconut 67
  Portuguese orange pudding 107
  sweet with anis 106

Duck
  braised with red cabbage 95-6

crispy steamed, with water chestnuts and mushrooms 117-18
  Welsh salt 95
  wild with ginger and port 128-9
Dumplings Salzburg 99

Eggs
  poached on a bed of tomato
   with leak sauce 140-1
  scrambled with saffron 156
  wrapped with lamb 54
Endive with mustard 148
Escovitch — Escabeche —
  Caveach 86

Falafel from Israel 14
Fennel and mimosa salad 30
Fish fillets wrapped in lettuce 117

Ginger sponge with pears 18
Gnocchi with parsley butter
  sauce 58
Gravlaks 70-1
Guinea fowl
  breast grilled with orange and
   lime 57
  with green peppercorns 71

Haddock with mangoes and
  coconut 40
Herring, salted, gratin
  Swedish style 14
Hot lime pickle 89-90
Hungarian platter steak 80-1

Ice cream

layered cake 125
strawberry and rose petal 131

Jasmine cream with mint
jelly 143
Jelly
mint with Jasmine cream 143
muscat with muscat grapes 131
Northern fruit 98-9
Junket and prune whip 119

Kid leg roasted Tuscan style 15

Lamb
kidneys in baked potato
jackets 15
korma with spinach 16
loin with mushrooms 122-3
best end aux herbes de
Provence 112
Leeks
with lemon and sugar 18
with peppers, tomatoes, garlic
and anchovy 157
Lemon
and brazil nut soup 46
curd tart 113
pickled in the Arab fashion 50
Lime pickle 89-90
Liquorice ginger bread 124-5
Lobster
in a top hat 156-7
Portuguese style 105
Loganberry kissel 99

Mackerel
with gooseberry sauce 102-3
smoked in a brandade 55
Marmalade steamed pudding 27
Meatballs with yogurt and
caraway 87
Melon
and loganberries in Muscat
wine 119
sorbet with peaches 42-3
Meringue 67, 149
Meze 54-5
Mocha creams 74-5
Monkfish roast with black
pepper and port 152
Mushrooms
with garlic, parsley and red
wine 118
Magyar 81-2
stuffed Polish style 41-2
Mussels
Belgian style 86
deep fried with walnut and
sesame sauce 46

Omelette
Emperor's 75
Sister Abigail's blue flower 30
Persian herb 22

Sea urchin 78
Onion
bread ring 34-5
maple glazed 18
Orange
pudding Portuguese style 107
salad with cinnamon 42
Oysters
poached with julienne of
vegetables and champagne 152
Rockefeller 72-3
with red butter 103
with watercress cream 116-117

Pancakes
sweetcorn 64
spinach and sorrel 57-8
Passion fruit soufflé 153
Peaches
with chicken and cinnamon 24
with lemon and brandy 51
Pears with ginger sponge 18-19
Peas and ham 82
Peppers, yellow baked with
anchovies 48-9
Pheasant
braised with celery and port
123-4
braised with plums 129-30
with Norwegian cheese 71-2
sausages 156
Pistachio cream 153
Plum tart from Alsace 66-7
Pork
barbecued Tex-Mex 134-5
kebabs Balkan style 88
stir fried with cumin and
spinach 146
Potato
gratin 64-5
griddle cakes 17-18
hashed browns 33
Jansson's temptation 96
Paprikash 81
sour salad 88-9
Swiss cheese croquettes 22
with mint and garlic 42
Prawn
balls with tamarind sauce 94-5
giant, with ginger and dill 86-7
sour soup 62
Prune pudding Norwegian style
75

Ratatouille, New World 135-6
Red Mullet with pimentos 31
Rice pudding with orange
flower and rose conserve 35

Salads
avocado and cucumber 42
blue cheese 73
chicken and cucumber 62-3
chickpea, tomato and onion
with yoghurt 130

courgettes and mint with eggs 38
cucumber 73
fennel and mimosa 30
Japanese asparagus 62
mixed shellfish with tomato and
onion 38-9
North African 16-17
salsify with red dressing 146-8
sour potato 88-9
sweet-sour carrots 50
tomato 96-7
yellow flower with goat cheese
toast 110
Salads, fruit
orange with cinnamon 42
West Indian fruit 91
winter fruit in red wine 131
Sandwich spread from Eastern
Europe 18
Satsuma gratin 51
Scallops grilled with Szechwan
pepper 102
Sea urchin omelette 78
Seafood gumbo 70
Shark with lemon 134
Shellfish
pilaff as in Marseille 15-16
salad with tomato and onion
38-9
Shortbread, Polish, with red
fruit filling 19
Shrimp remoulade 70
Smoked mackerel brandade 55
Smoked salmon and caviar rolls
31
Sole simmered in sake 64
Sorbet
melon with peaches 42-3
orange with strawberries 153
tangerine 26-7
Soufflé
layered citrus 148-9
passion fruit 153
Soups
banana curry 140
carrot and coriander 30
cold almond 128
cold beetroot 22-3
cold yoghurt 22
crab bisque 38
green 94
lemon and brazil nut 46
sour prawn 62
tomato and red pepper 134
tomato, orange and cardamom
78-9
Spinach
and prunes spiced 96
and sorrel pancakes 57-8
semisweet tart with raisins and
pine kernels 130-1
Spring rolls with peanut sauce
65-6
Squab
grilled Tuscan style 79

stir fried with mange tout peas
63
stuffed with apricots 141
Squid Veneziana stewed in its
own ink 39
Strawberries
and oranges in Asti Spumante
107
and redcurrants 43
and rose petal ice cream 131
dipped in chocolate with cream
and pineapple 19
with black pepper and orange
sherbet 153
Sicilian cream 26
tart 143
Sweetcorn
pancakes 64
with pimento 135
Sweetmeats
for Concerians 43
Mediterranean 107

Tapenade 55
Taramasalata 55
Tart
artichoke 128
lemon curd 113
plum from Alsace 66-7
semisweet spinach 130-1
strawberry 143
Tomato
orange and cardamom soup 78-9
and red pepper soup 134
salad 96-7
stuffed with cream cheese and
basil 14
Turbot cooked in cider 104-05
Turkey
breast with four spices 32-3
escalopes with lemon and
parsley 47-8
Turnips glazed 141-3

Veal escalopes with Parmesan
cheese and Parma ham 23
Vegetables with lemon and oil
73-4
Violet pudding 35

Walnut
cake with figs and cream 58-9
stuffed with marzipan and
caramelized 27
Watermelon rind pickled 118-19

Yoghurt 59

Zucchini
and carrot with mint sauce
112-13
and mint salad with eggs 38